PRAISE FOR *LAS*

"Carey has become one of the most prominent and needed voices in church leadership today. I think the reason we read and listen to him so much is he is balanced, wise, and incredibly practical. This is not just another book — here is one you can read quickly, but immediately begin to implement and grow a stronger church. Thanks again, Carey! You're making a difference."

—RON EDMONDSON, BLOGGER AND
SENIOR PASTOR OF IMMANUEL BAPTIST CHURCH

"I believe churches should grow because every number has a name. At the same time, church growth is personal for leaders, and that can be dangerous. When attendance is up, you feel good about yourself. When attendance is down, you think about going into another line of work. This is one of the many reasons I'm grateful Carey has written his book, Lasting Impact. It's practical advice for leaders who want to grow their church and remain emotionally healthy in the process."

—JEFF HENDERSON, LEAD PASTOR, GWINNETT CHURCH

"Carey is not only one of the most prolific thinkers of this generation, but one of the most practical. Lasting Impact is insightful and in a league of its own when it comes to applicability. This book gives you the tools you need to make changes now! Regardless of the size of your church or team you lead, if you're wanting to reach higher heights, this book is a must read."

—Joshua Gagnon, Lead Pastor, Next Level Church

"Carey Nieuwhof is a voice you should listen to. As a senior pastor, he's been in the trenches of ministry, and combines both wisdom and practical application to provide an effective resource for church leaders at any level. If you're looking to grow your church, this book is a must read and must have on your leadership shelf. The conversations contained in this book are essential and much needed."

—Brad Lomenick, Former president of Catalyst and author of The Catalyst Leader and H3 Leadership

"There are people that talk about church growth and people who actually grow churches. Carey is the latter. Lasting Impact is a masterpiece of practical steps to reach your community for Jesus. Lasting Impact should be required reading for pastors."

—Casey Graham, Founder and CEO of The Rocket Company

"Very few people have the giftedness of my friend, Carey Nieuwhof. He has the ability to understand the importance and development of clarity, culture, processes, growth — all while communicating the purpose of the church. Lasting Impact has some of Carey's best leadership thoughts on these issues. He guides us on a journey where the health and effectiveness of our church becomes the destination."

—CALEB KALTENBACH, LEAD PASTOR, DISCOVERY CHURCH AND
AUTHOR OF MESSY GRACE

"For my money, no one speaks to the needs of today's pastor better than Carey Nieuwhof. A lot of people will give you opinions; Carey gives you practical solutions. Lasting Impact will not only answer the questions you're asking, it will answer the questions you should be asking."

—LANE JONES, DIRECTOR OF NORTH POINT
MINISTRIES STRATEGIC PARTNER GROUP

"In Lasting Impact, Carey points out issues that are often addressed too late and guides us down a path of conversations that are usually ended too quickly. We can all use more honest conversations in our leadership and this book provides a great place to start."

– FRANK BEALER, FAMILY PASTOR AT ELEVATION CHURCH

LASTING IMPACT:

SEVEN POWERFUL CONVERSATIONS
THAT WILL HELP YOUR CHURCH GROW

CAREY NIEUWHOF

LFAD PASTOR OF CONNEXUS CHURCH

LASTING IMPACT

7 POWERFUL CONVERSATIONS
THAT WILL HELP YOUR CHURCH GROW

Lasting Impact
Seven Powerful Conversations That Will Help Your Church Grow

Published by The reThink Group, Inc.
5870 Charlotte Lane, Suite 300
Cumming, GA 30040 U.S.A.

ISBN 978-1-941259-46-7

Photo: Cole Bennett Photography, Orillia Ontario
Project Management: Kevin Jennings, Joanna Easley, and Kristen Brady
Editor: Darcie Clemen
Cover Design: Hudson Phillips
Interior Design: Hudson Phillips, Julie Shefchunas, and Chris Sandlin

4 5 6 7 8 9 10 11 12 13

08/07/2018

To the leaders (staff and volunteer) who read my blog
and listen to my podcast.

*Your stories, struggles, and successes motivate me more than you
realize. It's an honor to be part of the conversation in your life
and around your leadership table.*

CONTENTS

ACKNOWLEDGEMENTS

As anyone who has written a book knows, writing is an exhilarating and exhausting process. This book had some of its genesis in early-morning writing sessions where the ideas first appeared as blog posts. But turning this into a book took more time than I expected. My wife, Toni, has been my best friend for more than twenty-five years, and she has put up with so many "I'm not quite done yet" moments of me writing that I lost count ages ago. Her steadfast encouragement, love, support, and patience are a little surreal at times, or at least divinely motivated. I couldn't imagine my life without her or without my sons, Jordan and Sam, and daughter-in-law, Alex, who also put up with a preoccupied dad at times. There's nothing quite as amazing as family, and I'm so grateful for mine.

I have an incredible congregation, staff team, and elder group at Connexus Church. It's a privilege to have discussed virtually all of the contents of the book with them long before I wrote any of it. I am so thankful that our staff and elders are open to change and are willing to think through the toughest issues we face as a church and culture. In addition, a special thanks to my assistant, Sarah Piercy, who puts together all the bits and pieces of my life into a coherent whole. Without her skill and heart for ministry, I'm not sure how I'd be able to do what I do.

Reggie Joiner and Andy Stanley are two leaders from whom I have learned so much over the last decade. Anyone who is familiar with their work will see their thinking has shaped mine (for the better), and I'm grateful for many conversations I've had with them that have ended up influencing the conversations around my leadership table. It's such a privilege to be part of the community at Orange and North Point.

There is a tremendous team behind this book. Joanna Easley provided very helpful project coordination as our team was spread out between several countries; she kept us all on track. Darcie Clemen has been a fantastic editor. Darcie took the original blog posts I wrote and put them together to form the spine of this book, stitching them together into an intelligent work. She also labored over the podcast transcripts and turned them into succinct written summaries with helpful insights. Her constant attention to detail through all the stages of writing made this book so much better. Kevin Jennings has been a tremendous asset. Kevin's creative and analytical mind shaped everything from the launch of my podcast to the redesign of my blog to the writing of this book and some future products you'll hear about in due time. He's committed to getting the message out to as many people as possible, and I'm so grateful for his hard work and input.

My wife, Toni; Elevation Church's Frank Bealer; and Connexus Church's Andy Harvey each gave extensive feedback on the manuscript that improved it. Ron Edmondson, Josh Gagnon, and Josh Pezold also read earlier versions of the manuscript and provided encouragement and feedback that helped tremendously. Casey Graham, Kevin Jennings, and about two thousand readers gave some incredibly helpful advice on titling the book (which has to be the most mysti-fying aspect of writing, at least for me).

Finally, thank you to all of you who have contributed to the ideas in this book by your comments and conversation around my blog, and podcast, and in the many conversations that happen at conferences when I'm traveling. Your ideas, questions, stories, and encouragement are a continual source of fuel. You have no idea how grateful I am for the courage with which you're leading.

INTRODUCTION

I love the local church. I mean *love* it. Nothing has the potential to change the world like the mission of the local church fully realized.

And yet, sometimes I wonder why Jesus chose the local church to accomplish his mission. I mean, I know how fickle and frail I am as a human being, and I've lived long enough to see how flawed the church can be. Couldn't Jesus come up with a better strategy? Like leading the church directly, without human intervention? Some days I think that would have been a much better approach. At least as far as I'm concerned.

But that's not what Jesus chose. He picked you. He picked me. He decided he was going to take all of his power, authority, strength, and love and pour them into people who, when banded together in the name of Jesus, form the church. That's pretty amazing, and doubtless is a sign of God's grace and deep love for humanity. If you're a church leader (staff or volunteer—there's really no distinction), you are one of millions of human beings whose normal lives have been disrupted by a call into the noblest and most fearsome of tasks: to share the hope of Jesus Christ with the world he so desperately loves.

As beautifully true as all of this is, it's also clear that the church in the Western world is at a crossroads. What was our reality just a few decades ago is no longer; we are swiftly moving into a post-Christian culture along with the tumble and confusion that accompany that shift. The challenges the church is facing today require our best leadership and our most faithful hearts. It's as incredibly exciting as it is daunting.

So what prompted this book? It has its beginning in both my blog and my podcast. In fact, the idea for the book sprang from the fact that numerous people told me they were using my articles or podcast episodes for team discussions in their churches. If you're a regular reader or listener, you'll recognize much of the material contained in the book. But you'll also see some significant differences.

Thinking in *book* is, in my view, different from thinking in *blog*. I've done a significant rewrite of the original blog source material and woven in a few of the insights from my leadership podcast to shape the conversation. (The podcast interviews in their entire form can be accessed for free on iTunes, Stitcher, or TuneIn Radio simply by searching for and subscribing to *The Carey Nieuwhof Leadership Podcast*.) Additionally, I've added discussion questions at the end of each chapter to help guide your team conversation.

What's the best way to read the book? You can certainly read it as a whole, cover to cover, but tackling all of these conversations at once as a team would be a bit daunting. When it comes to team conversations, I'd suggest choosing the conversation most relevant to your situation, working through it, and then picking another to tackle next. You may choose to have certain conversations and skip others. The book will work that way; I've intentionally left some overlap between some of the chapters for this reason.

In the end, I hope and pray this book will launch your team into a series of discussions that will not only help you lead better but also help you accomplish your mission more effectively. I believe teams that are willing to have open conversations about the most pressing challenges before the church today will have a lasting impact. In the future, the churches that grow will be the churches whose leaders courageously hold the most honest conversations and then take action. If this book helps with that in some small way, I will be incredibly grateful. Because, like you, I love the local church and its leaders.

Carey Nieuwhof
April 2015

WHY ARE WE NOT GROWING FASTER?

There's no question that church growth is a felt need among church leaders. I meet very few church leaders who hope their church actually declines in the next year. But before you stop at this first conversation, realize the other six conversations in this book are all tied to growth. Unhealthy churches won't grow. Churches that fail to release high-capacity leaders will struggle with growth. Churches that ignore the culture will always struggle. You'll see the pattern if you look.

Because growth is such a big issue, I'll cover a lot of ground in this chapter. We'll look at what to do if your church isn't growing and changes you can make to turn things around. You'll find some thought-provoking questions to discuss with your team and dig deeper. And finally, we'll take a serious look at what it takes to reach the unchurched and how you can be ready to do that. If you and your team want to get serious about growth, I believe these are the conversations you need to have.

SO THIS SUBJECT MIGHT BE A LITTLE SENSITIVE ...

Before we begin, please realize church growth is a paradoxical subject. Many church leaders dismiss church growth as being less important than discipleship, or are critical of those who they believe are overfocused on attendance. Yet if I showed you the traffic statistics page of the blog I write, you'd also see that by far (and I mean *by far*), the most accessed subject on my blog is church attendance and growth. Literally hundreds of thousands of leaders a year access those posts. It's the subject everyone wants to know about but no one wants to talk honestly about publicly.

Church growth can bring out a beast in some of us. We can overfocus on it. It can also distort our perception of ourselves. When our church is growing, it's easy to think we can do nothing wrong. And when we're not growing, it's easy to feel as if we do nothing right. Neither is healthy.

So why is growth a necessary subject around a leadership table? Because it's related to mission. My focus is not on growth for growth's sake, but for the sake of being effective in our mission and vision of reaching people who need to know the love of Christ in their lives. I'm passionate about church growth because the world is at its best when the church is at its best. I think almost every leader around your table could agree with that. So if the subject becomes emotional or unhealthy, come back to that central point. It's about the mission.

Even with that clarified, let me anticipate some of the other issues you might encounter in your team discussions. Often when church growth surfaces as a subject, some leaders will inevitably ask: "Well, what's wrong with small churches? Why are so many people obsessed with growth?" You might even have a few people go hyperspiritual and start quoting Scripture verses to justify why church growth is a bad thing.

Understand that most of us carry an innate sensitivity about certain subjects. For example, people often say my hair is blond, but I usually say it's red (it's kind of on the border). And for sure, my hair was red when I was a kid. It even came with freckles to boot. As you might appreciate, being redheaded in elementary school meant I got teased. That actually led to a schoolyard fight instigated by me in one of my not-very-awesome moments. At least kids stopped teasing me. Eventually, though, I grew past my sensitivity. By the time I became an adult, I didn't mind at all saying I had some ginger happening on my scalp.

I've noticed a similar defensiveness on the part of some church leaders when it comes to leading a small church or a church that's stalled out in growth, no matter what size. You might find the conversation gets heated and people start to defend the status quo ("we focus on *quality*, not quantity!"). That's natural ... but don't lose the mission in the midst of it. It's just too important. People need to be reached. The love of Jesus was designed to spill far beyond the walls of the church, not be contained within them.

Finally, don't be cynical about growing churches. That's just too easy. Sure, there are some driven leaders who are passionate about church growth because it makes *them* look good. God knows the hearts of people, and just because some people might want a church to grow because of ego does not mean all growth is bad.

As a rule, I believe that healthy things grow. Throughout the centuries, the mission of the church at its best has always been an outward mission focused on sharing the love Jesus has for the world with the world. That's why growth matters to me (and to so many of you).

CHURCH GROWTH IS A MYSTERY ... OR IS IT?

So how do churches grow? Some people would argue that it's mysterious. Maybe you just pray a lot. Or remain sincere. Or perhaps it's 100 percent up to God to determine which churches grow and which don't, and there's no formula you can use to make growth happen. Case closed.

I get that. And there's some truth in that. God is sovereign. Prayer matters, as does sincerity. And for sure, sometimes the people who lead growing churches are truly mystified as to why their church is growing. They can't give you specific reasons other than grace. On the one hand, that's absolutely true.

And yet, sometimes you and I make life out to be more mysterious than it actually is. For example, you might ask why you keep getting speeding tickets: *Why me, God?! Why?!* Yet the simple truth is, you usually speed. You might ask why your friendships are so conflicted when the reality is, you gossip. You wonder why your kids don't talk to you when, in fact, you were never around when they were young and don't really have much of a relationship with them as a result. Sometimes things aren't as mysterious as we make them out to be.

Take that a step further. Problems whose origins seem mysterious to us are often not that mysterious to others: we say we have a genetic predisposition toward gaining weight, but our coworkers see the fifth donut.

So maybe that's the case for those of us who want our church to reach new people but are puzzled by why that isn't happening. Perhaps it's not as mysterious as we think. There are traceable patterns in stagnant and declining churches as well as in healthy, growing churches. Spotting those patterns can help you spot your strengths and weaknesses. That's what the rest of this chapter is about.

First, we'll look at the patterns present in churches that aren't growing.

TEN REASONS YOUR CHURCH ISN'T GROWING (OR GROWING AS QUICKLY AS YOU'D LIKE)

What follows is a list of ten things that might be holding your church back from realizing the potential of its mission. The points that follow are, frankly, a bit blunt as well as short. But you'll figure out fairly quickly which apply and which don't. While we're often the last to see what so many others see, once someone names it, we're free to deal with it. In fact, among those who take it seriously and act, progress often ensues.

1. You're in conflict.

Ever been in someone's home as a guest only to have your hosts start to argue with each other? It doesn't happen that often, but the few times it's happened when I've been around have made me want to run out the door.

Why would church be any different? If you're constantly bickering and arguing, why would any new people stay? It's not that Christians shouldn't have conflict, but we should be the best in the world at handling it. The New Testament is a virtual manual of conflict resolution, but so many of us prefer gossip, nonconfrontation, and dealing with anyone but the party involved. How conflicted is your church—honestly? As long as you're conflicted, you'll have difficulty growing.

Growing churches handle conflict directly, biblically, humbly, and healthily.

2. You're more in love with the past than you are with the future.

This can be true of churches that are in love with tradition and churches that have had some amazing days recently. When leaders are more in love with the past than they are with the future, the end is near.

Many churches have frozen in their favorite era. Walk into some churches and it feels like 1949, 1970, 1996, or even 2005. The songs are dated, as is the approach. It's as if you've unearthed a time capsule. If your church is a museum of 1950 or even 2012, the likelihood of reaching the next generation diminishes with every passing day.

3. You're not that awesome to be around.

Fake. Judgmental. Hypocritical. Angry. Narrow. Unthinking. Unkind. Those are adjectives often used to describe Christians, and sometimes they have their basis in truth.

Alternatively, we all know certain people who are energizing to be around. You leave feeling better than when you came, simply because you were in their presence. Unfortunately, not enough Christians today fit that description. Jesus was mesmerizing. Paul caused conflict for sure, but he had many deep relationships and incredible influence. The early church was known for compassion and generosity.

If people truly don't want to be around you, don't let the reason be because you haven't let Christ reshape your character or social skills.

4. You're focused on yourself.

Too many churches are focused on their wants, preferences, and perceived needs. They are self-focused organizations filled with self-focused people. It should be no surprise that outsiders never feel welcomed, valued, or included. Sadly, if a person is self-focused, we call him or her selfish. If a church is self-focused, we call it normal.

If you want to reach people, however, you simply can't be self-focused. After all, a life devoted to self ultimately leaves you alone.

5. You think culture is the enemy.

If all you ever are is angry at the culture around you, how are you going to reach people in that culture? Christians who consistently expect non-Christians to act like Christians baffle me. If you treat your unchurched neighbor like an enemy, why would he ever want to be your friend? It is extremely difficult to impact people you don't actually like.

6. You're afraid to risk what is for the sake of what might be.

Let's face it: at least your church has *something* going for it. You're paying the bills. You have more people in your church than the churches around you that have closed. In fact, you can likely point to some programs in your church you might call a success, even if the success is only moderate. Which is exactly why you're struggling with the fear that virtually all of us struggle with: you're afraid to risk what is for the sake of what might be. That only gets worse, by the way, the more successful you become. The greatest enemy of your future success is your current success.

When you're perpetually afraid to risk what is for the sake of what might be, you may as well cue the funeral music now.

7. You can't make a decision.

Governance is a silent killer in today's churches. When your decision making is rooted in complex bureaucracy or congregational approval for every major change, it makes decision making difficult and courageous change almost impossible. Effective churches develop governance that is nimble;

is aligned around a common mission, vision,
and strategy;

trusts staff to accomplish the mission; and

has minimal congregational involvement in
decision making.

While that might be a surprise to some church leaders (perhaps even heresy to others), top-heavy, interventionist boards
and committees don't scale and won't allow staff leaders to
be as agile as they need to be to accomplish what they must
accomplish. Your governance might be killing you. And if it
takes you five layers of meetings to even decide whether that's
the case, you have a very serious problem indeed.

8. You talk more than you act.

Most church leaders love to think and love to debate issues,
which is great. Thoughtful leaders do that. But effective leaders add one more component. They *act*.

Most church leaders I know (staff and boards) overthink
and underact. If you acted on even a few more of your good
ideas, you could possibly be twice as effective in a very short
time frame. A B-plus plan brilliantly executed beats an A-plus
plan that never gets implemented, every single time.

9. You don't think there's anything wrong with
   your church.

I still run into a surprising number of leaders and church members who love their church but can't figure out why no one else does. What are other people saying that you're missing? Church leaders who think there's nothing wrong are on their way to soon having not much more to lead than a stalled-out club for the already convinced.

10. You're more focused on growth than you are
   on God.

Some leaders get so jacked up about growth that they forget it's about God and his mission. This is a danger every motivated leader needs to keep in mind. We're leading people to Jesus, not to ourselves or to our awesome church. Keeping the focus on Christ ensures that genuine life change happens and lasts.

Okay, so maybe this list stings a bit. Acknowledging the truth isn't easy for anyone. But I think being honest with yourself is the first step toward lasting change. If you're honest about where your church falls within these reasons, you'll be primed to make a meaningful change.

So where do you go next? Here are a few changes you can make.

STRUCTURE BIGGER TO GROW BIGGER

After you've honestly reviewed some of the reasons your church isn't growing or isn't growing quickly, there's still more ground to cover. Some churches begin to grow but simply can't keep up with the growth. The reasons, again, aren't nearly as mysterious as they are structural. In fact, what I talk about in this section in all likelihood applies to about 90 percent of the readers of this book. Why? While most media (social and traditional) are preoccupied with megachurches and multisite churches, the reality is that most churches in North America are quite small. The Barna Group reports that the average Protestant church size in America is 89 adults. Sixty percent of protestant churches have fewer than 100 adults in attendance. Only 2 percent have more than 1,000 adults attending.[1]

So what gives? Why is it that 90 percent of churches can't sustain growth beyond the 200 attendance mark? I promise you, in many cases it's not:

> *desire*—most leaders I know want their church to reach more people.
>
> *a lack of prayer*—many small church leaders are incredibly faithful in prayer.
>
> *love*—some of the people in smaller churches love people as authentically as anyone I know.
>
> *facility*—growth can start in the most unlikely places.

So let's just assume you have a solid mission, theology, and heart to reach people. You know why most churches still don't push past the 200 mark in attendance? It's because they organize, behave, lead, and structure themselves like *small* organizations. And any leader of a larger church knows that. In fact, churches that have passed the 200 barrier have also realized they've had to restructure and reorganize at 400, at 800, at 1,000, and again many times beyond that. Multisite churches even realize that moving to five sites creates far more organizational complexity than it does to move from one to two. If you want to grow bigger, you need to structure bigger.

Take yourself out of the church world for a moment, and you'll realize you recognize this principle intuitively in many areas of life. (For some reason we've come to believe erroneously it doesn't apply in the church.) For example, all of us know there's a world of difference between how you organize a corner store and how you organize a larger supermarket.

In a corner store, Mom and Pop run everything. Want to talk to the CEO? She's stocking shelves. Want to see the director of marketing? He's at the cash register. Mom and Pop do it all, and they organize their business to stay small. Which is fine if you're Mom and Pop and don't want to grow.

But you can't run a supermarket that way. You organize differently. You govern differently. You hire a produce manager and people who only stock shelves. You employ floor managers, shift managers, a general manager, and so many more. So what's the translation to the church world? What can you do to position yourself for growth? There are six moves you can make that will help.

1. Rethink the pastor's role.

In most small congregations, the pastor is the primary caregiver. Congregations expect it, and seminaries train leaders for it. But it's also what stifles the growth potential of almost every church. Think about it: when the pastor has to visit every sick person, do every wedding and funeral and make regular house calls, attend every meeting, and lead every Bible study or group, he or she becomes incapable of doing almost anything else. Message preparation falls to the side, and providing organizational leadership for the future is almost out of the question.

The pastoral care model of church leadership simply doesn't scale. It's somewhat ironic, actually. If you're a good pastoral care person, people will often love you so much that the church will grow to two hundred people, at which point the pastoral care expectations become crushing. Inevitably, pastoral leaders with larger churches can't keep up and end up disappointing people when they can't get to every event anymore. Additionally, many burn out under the load. The pastoral care model creates many false and unsustainable expectations. Consequently, almost everyone (congregation and leaders) gets hurt in the process.[2]

One answer to this dilemma is to teach people to care for each other in groups.[3] It's a model of care and leadership that goes back to Exodus 18, when Jethro confronted Moses about doing everything himself. Even Jesus adopted it, moving his disciples into groups of seventy, twelve, three, and then one.

In addition to modifying the care model, there's another complicating factor. Many pastors I know are people-pleasers by nature. Not wanting to disappoint people fuels conflict within leaders. So how do you deal with this? Go see a counselor. Get on your knees. Do whatever you need to do to get over the fear of disappointing people. Courageous leadership is like courageous parenting. Don't do what your kids want you to do; do what you believe is best for them in the end. Eventually, many of them will thank you. And the rest? Honestly, they'll probably go to another church that isn't reaching many people either.

2. Develop a strategy.
In addition to a new structure, growing churches develop a carefully thought-out strategy. Many churches today are clear on mission and vision. What most lack is a widely shared and agreed-upon strategy. Your vision and mission answer the *why* and *what* of your organization. Your strategy answers *how*. And don't kid yourself; *how* is critical. Spend time working through your strategy. Be clear on *how* you will accomplish your mission, and don't rest until the mission, vision, and strategy reside in every single volunteer and leader.

3. Let leaders lead.
Many small churches are not led by true leaders. Why? Well, in every church there are people who hold the position of leadership, and then there are people who are truly leaders (who may not hold any position in the church). Maybe they got into a seat of leadership because they've been there a long time or because no one else was willing. But holding a seat of leadership without having the gift of leadership is a strategy

for stagnation and dysfunction.

Consequently, one of the transitions every growing church makes involves moving people with the gift of leadership into positions of leadership. Similarly, effective churches will gently but firmly release people from positions of power when they hold titles but aren't advancing the mission.

How do you know who the real leaders are? A few things can help. First, check to see if anyone's following them. Second, look for godly people who have a track record of handling responsibility in other areas of life humbly but capably. Finally, look for people who have created momentum wherever they've gone and who possess wisdom. Then give them the job of leading the church into the future with you. If you actually have leaders leading, it will make a huge difference.

4. Empower your volunteers.

Sure, small churches may not have the budget to hire many staff, but every church has people who are more than capable of serving. Empower them. Volunteers that merely do as they are told out of a sense of duty will never contribute like those who own the vision, mission, and strategy and have been given the authority to lead. Once you have identified true leaders, and once you're clear on your mission, vision, and strategy, you need to release people to accomplish it. Try to do it all yourself, and you will burn out, leave, or simply be ineffective. Empower volunteers around an aligned strategy, and you will likely begin to see progress.

5. Stop micromanaging.

We've already seen that poor governance is a stumbling block to growth. The biggest obstacle in this regard is a board that feels they need to micromanage. If you need permission every time you need to buy paper towels or repaint an office, you have a governance issue. Most boards who micromanage do so because that's all they've ever known. Or because there's a lack of trust. The board of an effective church will guard the mission and vision (holding leaders accountable), empower the team to accomplish the mission and vision, and get out of the way of day-to-day management.[4]

6. Simplify your programming.

Most churches are doing too much, or at least attempting to do too many things. When I began in ministry, as a seminary student, I led three small churches with a grand total of forty-five people in attendance. We had eighteen elders between the three tiny churches. Overall, the church was in evening meetings two to three times a week. We also added numerous bake sales, bazaars, and fund-raising dinners into the mix because the church had little money. Why on earth would a church that small be that busy? Why on earth would we need to meet that often? And why didn't people just tithe? Do you know how many cookies you need to sell to make $500?

We eventually repurposed most of those meetings to become meetings about vision and reorganization. Then we radically cut down our ministry programming, killing some long-standing programs and replacing them with a few targeted ministries that would help us best accomplish our mission. We also cut down the number of elders. The resulting streamlined ministry gave people a few well-chosen options rather than a large menu of random programs that led nowhere in particular. Also, the smaller governance structure made for more agile decision making, allowing a more responsive and change-ready approach to leadership. Now, although I lead a much bigger church of one thousand weekly attenders, I'm out only half a dozen nights a month or less (including small group).

Activity does not equal accomplishment. Just because you're busy doesn't mean you're being effective. If you have a lot of programs that accomplish little and lead nowhere, stop them. Yes, people will be mad. Muster the courage to cut some good programs; good is the enemy of great. Then go out and do a few great things. Free up your time so you and your team can accomplish something truly significant.

Structuring bigger to grow bigger is as painful and difficult as it is necessary. But it's also liberating and freeing. Sure, it may be radical. But radical problems demand radical solutions.

SO THERE'S NO SILVER BULLET?

Somewhere in your team discussion you'll be tempted to believe that this has to be simpler. Maybe you'll try to convince yourself that you really would grow if you only had one or two more things to make your ministry thrive. For example, maybe you've said any combination of these things:

"We would grow if we …

… got out of our portable location and opened a new building."

… got out of our current building and became portable." (I've actually talked with leaders who think they would grow explosively if they left their old building and became portable.)

… added new technology (like lights, sound, or video)."

… merged with another church."

… added a new campus."

And would you?

Here's my theory: no, you wouldn't. Before you get discouraged, let me explain why this line of thinking rarely, if ever, works. David Ogilvy, the famous 20th century advertising guru, is well known for saying that great marketing just makes a bad product fail faster. That's the principle most of us want to ignore, or at least I do.

Most churches aren't held back because of their venue or even because of their technology. They're stagnant or dying because they're not connecting with people and effectively fulfilling their mission. The trap most leaders fall into is believing that *a change in form will be an adequate substitute for a change in substance.* But a change in form *never* makes up for a change in substance. Substantive change is the only thing that will truly change the trajectory of most churches and organizations.

A change in venue won't help a dying church grow.

Better media won't help a dying church grow.

Adding new campuses won't help a dying church grow.

Merging won't help two or three dying churches grow.

I've lived through this tension. In less than two decades, our church has met in a century-old building, an elementary school, a new facility, a movie theater, and once again in a brand-new facility. Through all phases, we've grown from a handful of people to just over one thousand on weekends today. And throughout, buildings, technologies, and even locations have been means to an end, not ends in themselves. They did not *make* us grow or reach new people. They *helped*, but they are not the secret sauce.

HOW TO MAKE THINGS WORSE

Sometimes leaders can end up making the situation worse without even realizing how it happened. So, in the interest of clarity, if you want to make things worse, here's how to do it: Address form, but don't address substance. Never resolve your underlying problems. Instead, add technology, add locations, add campuses, or engineer a merger, and hope that all this will solve all your problems. It will not.

In fact, it will make them worse. Because now, instead of being in your old building with a manageable budget, you are in a new one with higher costs you can't pay. Instead of having a simple message people can understand, you have all this technology that is creating even greater distance between you and the people you're trying to reach. Instead of being in one location, you are in two, only to discover you now have momentum issues in two locations. Or, if you arrange a merger, you now have two organizations' problems to solve. (This is why church mergers in mainline churches almost never work. Church *takeovers* can and do work, by the way.)

I believe these things are true: You can grow a church in a centuries-old building. And you can kill a church in a brand-new, multimillion-dollar facility. You can grow a church with zero media. And you can waste a million dollars on lights, gear, and cameras. You can grow a church in a single site. And you can go bankrupt adding venues no wants to come to. These truths are hard truths, but they're helpful because they make us look in the mirror and get on our knees. They help us realize where the issue really is and make us do the homework and the heartwork we need to do.

Please hear me. I have led church mergers *and* multisite expansions *and* building campaigns *and* a portable church *and* rapid technological change in the church, and they've all *helped* us reach more people and grow our ministry. But I think it's only because we sat down and solved our underlying problems as an organization *first*. As we got healthier inwardly, we grew outwardly. We tackled the issues of substance *before* and as often as possible even as we tackled the issues of form.

And (don't miss this) God has been incredibly gracious to us. (I say that just so you know that I'm not trying to take credit.) And God has been gracious to you, too, I'm sure. It's just that God's grace is no substitute for using your mind and heart to engage the issues of leadership that are before you. For us, the whole journey started with prayer, Scripture, and a burning desire to reach people who were far from God. Then we figured out a strategy to help us accomplish that. Twenty years into the leadership journey for me, it still starts with prayer, Scripture, and a burning desire.

BUT WE'RE STILL NOT GROWING ...

So what if you've reorganized, strategized, and made substantive changes in your church, but you're still not growing? Almost every church (and almost every organization) faces seasons in which growth stops. Some haven't seen growth in years ... or decades.

One of the best things any leader can do when he or she in a tough spot is to stop making assumptions and start asking questions. Our assumptions got us to where we are, but they won't necessarily get us where we need to go. I've found four questions in particular are helpful when your church stops growing.

1. Is our sense of mission white hot?

Effective churches have a white hot sense of mission. It's far more than a piece of paper on a wall or something the board recites at annual meetings; it lives daily in the souls of countless people in the congregation. It motivates all the action in the organization. It consumes people.

Often a church that has stopped growing has lost the urgency behind its mission. This is doubly sad in the case of a church because our mission is actually Christ's mission— it's the spreading of the gospel into the world for which Jesus died.

Leaders and congregations that are effective in accomplishing their mission are consumed by their mission. It always burns white hot.

2. Has our strategy or approach become dated?

While the mission of the church is eternal, strategy should shift from generation to generation. Today it needs to shift even more quickly than that. You may have skipped through the strategy section earlier in this chapter and thought, *That's okay ... we have a highly developed strategy.* That may be true. But is your strategy still effective, or is it dated?

Identifying a dated strategy is easy if you're a new leader who has taken over from someone else. It is much harder when you've led in a context for more than five years. The challenge in long-term leadership is that the changes that you introduced may have been novel and effective when you introduced them, but it's not 1995 anymore, or 2005, for that matter.

How do you tell if your strategy is dated? When it stops being effective. Another clue is when you see very few people in the next generation adopting the approach or strategy in question. Tomorrow's leaders tend to gravitate toward tomorrow's solutions. Make sure you understand where the next generation is heading in terms of their strategy. Better yet, get them around your table.

3. Are we on top of the constant change in our culture?

While you're studying your strategy, you might also want to study culture. It's changing, radically and quickly. I believe when historians look back on our generation, they will see it as a crack in history. We now live in a post-Christian, post-modern world. That's true in Canada. It's increasingly true in the United States. In my experience, many of us in church leadership don't really grasp the enormity of the change going on around us. If you want to explore more of this conversation, chapter 6 is dedicated to exploring the changing trends in our culture.

4. Are we focused on unchurched people or on ourselves?

There's a tendency you and I have as human beings. Our natural drift is to focus on ourselves. Not on Christ. Not on others. The gravitational pull of any church is toward insiders, not outsiders. Left unattended, your church will become a place where the preferences of the members trump passion for the mission. There are two primary ways to address this drift:

> In every decision, focus on who you want to reach, not on who you want to keep.

Commit to losing yourself for the sake of finding others.

I completely understand that people automatically respond with, "Well, what about me and my needs (or the needs of our faithful members)?" Jesus said something about finding your life in the process of losing it (Matthew 10:39). People who focus on helping others and honoring Christ soon discover that their needs are met far more deeply than they ever experienced otherwise.

NOW YOU'RE READY TO REACH THE UNCHURCHED

So now that the problems have been diagnosed, what are some signs you're ready to reach unchurched people—ready to throw the doors open? Growing churches have often embraced the following characteristics:

Your main services engage teenagers. I've talked with many church leaders who want to reach unchurched people but can't understand why unchurched people don't like their church. They are stumped until I ask them one last question: Do the teens in your church love your services and want to invite their friends? As soon as I asked that question, the leader's expression would inevitably change. He or she would look down at the floor and say no. Here's what I believe: if teens find your main services (yes, the ones you run on Sunday mornings) boring, irrelevant, and disengaging, so will unchurched people. As a rule, if you can design services that engage teenagers, you've designed a church service that engages unchurched people.

You're good with questions. This one's still hard for me. I like to think that every question has an answer. I think one of the reasons unchurched people flee churches is that they feel shut down when every question they ask has a snappy or quick answer.

They will find answers, but you need to give them time. Embracing the questions of unchurched people is a form of embracing them.

You're honest about your struggles. Unchurched people get suspicious when church leaders and Christians appear to have it "all together." Let's face it: you don't. And they know it. When you are honest about your struggles, it draws unchurched people closer. I make it a point to tell unchurched people that our church isn't perfect, that we will probably let them down, but that one of the marks of a Christian community is that we can deal with our problems face-to-face and honestly, and that I hope we will be able to work it through. There is a strange attraction to that.

You have easy, obvious, strategic, and helpful steps for new people. I am a fan of steps, not programs.[5] One sure sign that you are ready to handle an influx of unchurched people is that your church has a clear, easily accessible pathway to move someone from their first visit right through to integration with existing Christians in small groups or other core ministries. Most churches simply have randomly assembled programs that lead nowhere in particular.

You've dumped all assumptions. It's easy to assume that unchurched people "must know" at least the basics of the Christian faith. Lose that thinking. How much do you (really) know about Hinduism or Taoism? That's about how much many unchurched people (really) know about Christianity. Don't fight it. Embrace it. Make it easy for everyone to access what you are talking about whenever you are talking about it.

Your outreach isn't just a program. Many Christians think having a "service" for unchurched people or a program designed for unchurched people is enough. It's not. When you behave as if reaching unchurched people can be done through a program or an alternate service, you're building a giant brick wall for unchurched people to walk into. You might as well tell them, "This *program* is for you, but our *church* is for us. Sorry."

You are flexible and adaptable. In the future, you will not "arrive." I think the approach to unchurched people and the strategy behind the mission of the church needs to be flexible and adaptable. Don't design a "now we are done" model for reaching unchurched people. You may never be done. Churches that are adaptable and flexible in their strategy (not in their mission or vision) will have the best chance of continually reaching unchurched people. "How quickly can your church change?" will become a defining question of future churches.[6]

Three Causes of Decline

While the causes of church stagnation and decline are complex, they essentially fall into three categories:

1. Internal dysfunction that is sapping the community of its life, such as conflict; wrong people in wrong places; unrealistic expectations of staff, boards, and volunteers.

2. Structural issues, such as boards that micromanage or pastoral care being vested in one or a handful of leaders.

3. An inward focus that refuses to acknowledge the need to change to be effective with outsiders.

Churches that deal with these internal issues will be in a much better position to deal with the subject of chapter 6. It discusses the cultural change happening around us that's making it more difficult for even healthier churches to grow.

Conversation #1

DISCUSSION QUESTIONS

Talk About It

1. Has the subject of why churches grow seemed mysterious to you? Why or why not?

2. Of the ten reasons churches don't grow listed on pages 6–10, which (if any) resonate as being true in your context?

3. Is your church restructuring to grow bigger, or is it run more like a "mom-and-pop" operation?

4. To what extent do you think the pastor's role needs to be redefined in your church? How would you redefine it?

5. Has your church or leadership team ever fallen into "silver-bullet" thinking about church growth? How can silver-bullet thinking harm a church team?

6. Is your sense of mission white hot? If so, how have you kept it that way? If not, what would it take to ignite your sense of mission?

Get Practical

1. What specific structural changes does your team need to make this year to grow bigger? What changes should you make next year?

2. Read through the key points on pages 25–27, "Now You're Ready to Reach the Unchurched." How many of the seven characteristics listed accurately describe you? Make a list of what needs to change.

Make It Happen

Identify your single biggest obstacle to growth as a church. Once you've identified it, create a six-month plan to remove it.

In addition, identify two to five other key obstacles to growth. Now design a one- to two-year plan to address each of the obstacles.

Make sure you assign responsibilities and accountability and meet periodically to evaluate progress.

HOW DO WE RESPOND AS PEOPLE ATTEND CHURCH LESS OFTEN?

In chapter 1, we talked about how you can make a lot of internal change but still struggle to see your church grow. Maybe that's where you are as a church. You're basically healthy, your church is structured for growth, and you are committed to reaching people outside your walls, but you're sensing that growth and even effectiveness in your mission are more difficult than they used to be.

You're not alone. What you'll discover, even if you're successful in leading more people than ever before into a relationship with Jesus, is that people are simply attending church less frequently. Everywhere I go I talk to pastors who are experiencing the same thing: *people who attend church are attending less often*. People who used to attend every week are attending three times a month. People who were around twice a month often now show up once a month or less. And attenders who used to come once a month are showing up half a dozen times a year. This is true of rapidly growing churches, megachurches, midsized churches, and Bible churches. It's a massive cultural shift.

It's interesting how quickly things have shifted. When I started in ministry in the mid-90s, if someone didn't attend church for a while, it was almost always because they had left. It made running into people in the grocery store a bit awkward, as they really didn't want to tell you they had moved on. Today when I run into people I haven't seen at our church in weeks or months, they tell me they *love* our church and that they can't wait to get back at some point. It doesn't even occur to them that in the recent past someone might have guessed they left. They haven't left at all; they just haven't been lately.

In this chapter, we'll look at some reasons that's happening and then begin to plot out a strategy, first looking at the characteristics of today's unchurched people and infrequent attenders (they're quite similar), and then at some more practical suggestions of how to approach and engage people. Please know this is a relatively new conversation in many church circles. That's compounded by the fact that our culture is changing faster than ever before as we move from a Christian culture to a post-Christian culture in North America. That said, I believe it's incredibly important to *have* this conversation anyway. New and innovative approaches will emerge from these conversations that will move the mission forward in a new generation. So I encourage you to have the conversation despite its lack of definition. I hope this chapter will provide a framework for it and some food for thought.

Let me clarify two things first. Yes, the church is bigger than simply Sunday mornings, but this chapter focuses on the issue of church service attendance. Second, mere church *attendance* is never the goal. But attendance is a sign of something deeper that every church leader is going to have to wrestle with over the next few years. And it continues to be a pivotal part of how the church in the West gathers even today.

11 REASONS WHY EVEN COMMITTED CHURCH ATTENDERS ARE ATTENDING LESS OFTEN

The first key to addressing what's happening is to *understand* what's happening.

Why are even committed attenders attending less often? There are at least eleven reasons.

1. Greater Affluence

Money gives people options. If your church is engaging the middle class, the upper middle class, or a suburban demographic at all, an interesting trend is developing. The middle class is shrinking, but it's shrinking (in part) because more of the middle class is becoming *upper* class.[7] Both U.S. and Canadian personal disposable incomes are at all-time highs.[8] There are simply more affluent people than there were decades ago, which may in part explain why so many "average" people indulge their obsessions with granite countertops, designer homes, and new cars, even without being megawealthy.

Naturally, this leaves a huge theological void in ministry to and with the poor, but it helps explain what's actually happening in the suburbs and increasingly with the reurbanization of many cities as the affluent move back downtown. Please, I'm not arguing that things *should* be this way. I'm simply pointing out that this seems to be what's happening.

Again, people with money have options: for technology, for travel, and for their kids. And, arguably, that affluence may be one of the factors moving them further away from a committed engagement to the mission of the local church. It's perhaps fueling some of the other reasons outlined below.

2. Increased Focus on Kids' Activities

A growing number of kids are playing sports. And a growing number of kids are playing on teams that require travel. Many of those sports happen on weekends, and affluent parents are choosing sports over church.

3. More Travel

Despite a wobbly economy, travel is on the rise, both for business and for pleasure.[9]

More and more families of various ages travel for leisure, even if it's just out of town to go camping, visit friends, or spend a weekend at the lake. And when people are out of town, they tend not to be in church. This is true not just for families and business travelers but also for retired adults. Travel has quickly become a staple of many people's retirement plans.

4. A 24-7 Culture

Having to "work the weekend" was unusual a few decades ago, but now it's normal for a growing number of workers.

Weekend shift work is no longer just normal for emergency and health care workers; factory workers, retail workers, and even some white-collar workers work weekends. We have become a 24-7 culture. The idea of a common pause day—let alone a Sabbath—is a distant memory.

Although Sunday morning is still arguably the best time of the week to gather a crowd, Sunday mornings do not provide the universal opportunity they used to provide.

5. Blended and Single-Parent Families

Fortunately, more and more blended families and single-parent families are finding a home in church. So how does this translate into attendance patterns? Church leaders need to remember that when custody is shared in a family situation, "perfect" attendance for a kid or teen might be twenty-six Sundays a year. Similarly, while the affluent might not be in church because of *access* to reliable transportation, single parents (who, not always, but often struggle more financially) might not be in church because they *lack access* to reliable transportation.

So here's the strange twist. People who *have* a car are often not in church *because* they have a car. People who *want* to be in church are often *not* in church because they *don't* have a car or because it's not their "weekend" for church. Sadly, many people who want to get to church simply can't.

6. Online Options

Churches are also launching online campuses that bring the entire service to you on your phone, tablet, or TV. Churches that may not have the resources to create an entire online campus or experience are still establishing a social media presence. Many also podcast their messages. As we'll see later in this chapter and again in chapter 6, there are pros and cons to online church, and there's also little doubt that churches with a strong online presence have seen it negatively impact physical attendance (but likely increase their reach). Whether or not your church has online options doesn't make the issue go away. Anyone who attends your church has free access to any online ministry of any church. Online church is here to stay, whether you participate in it or not.

7. The Cultural Disappearance of Guilt

When I grew up, I felt guilty about not being in church on a Sunday. The number of people who feel guilty about not being in church on Sunday shrinks daily. As I mentioned earlier, I regularly meet people who haven't been in months but say they *love* our church. If you're relying on guilt as a motivator, you need a new strategy. (Well, honestly, you've always needed a new strategy.) Unchurched people don't feel any more guilty about not being in church on Sunday than you feel guilty about not being in synagogue on Saturdays. How many Saturdays do you feel bad about missing synagogue? That's how many Sundays they feel bad about missing church.

8. Self-Directed Spirituality

People are looking less to churches and leaders to help them grow spiritually and more to other options. We live in an era in which no parent makes a visit to a doctor's office without having first Googled the symptoms of a child's illness and a recommended course of treatment. Just ask any family physician. It drives them crazy. (Google, doctors will tell you, is not a complete replacement for medical school.) Similarly, when was the last time you bought a car without completely researching it online? In an age when we have access to everything, more and more people are self-directing their spirituality—for better or for worse.

Similarly, another characteristic of the postmodern mind is a declining trust of and reliance on institutions. The church in many people's minds is seen as an institution. I don't actually believe that's what a church is; I think it's a movement, not an institution. But many churches behave like institutions, and the postmodern mind instinctively moves away from them and toward a personalized spirituality as a result.

9. Failure to See a Direct Benefit

People always make time for the things they value most. If they're not making time for church, that tells you something. Even among people who say they love the church and who say they love *your* church, if declining attendance is an issue, chances are it's because they don't see a direct benefit. They don't see the value in attending church week after week. That could be because there isn't much value (gut check). Or it could be because there is value that they simply don't see.

Either way, failure to see a direct benefit always results in declining engagement.

So what are you doing or not doing that leaves people feeling there's not that much value?

10. Valuing Attendance Over Engagement

When someone merely *attends* church, the likelihood of showing up regularly or even engaging their faith decreases over time. At our church, I find our most engaged people—people who serve, give, invite, and who are in a community group—are our most frequent attenders. More and more as a leader, I value engagement over attendance. Ironically, leaders who value attendance over engagement will see declining attendance.

11. A Massive Culture Shift

All of these trends witness to something deeper. Our culture is shifting. Seismically.

Church leaders who fail to recognize this will not be able to change rapidly enough to respond to the shifts that are happening. Change is unkind to the unprepared, so prepare.

CHARACTERISTICS OF TODAY'S UNCHURCHED PERSON

Teams that truly want to connect with infrequent attenders and unchurched people need to come to terms with how radically mind-sets are changing as our culture is changing. There are a few books that do a great job outlining the shifting mind-set in great detail; it's perhaps helpful here to outline a few of the shifts that have been observed.[10]

In my two decades in ministry, I've seen a big shift in how unchurched people think. Perhaps the view in Canada is a little different from that in other regions in North America. Canada is a bit of a hybrid between the United States and Europe. Canadians are less churched and more post-Christian than many Americans but less secular than Europeans. Postmodernism has a deeper foothold here than in almost any place in America except perhaps the Northwest and New England, where it might be about the same. The characteristics outlined below challenge assumptions that many church leaders have held (or still hold) about how infrequent attenders or unchurched people feel about themselves and about the church.

They don't all have big "problems." If you're waiting for unchurched people to show up because their lives are falling apart, you might wait a long time. Sure, there are always people in crisis who seek God out. But many are quite content with their lives without God. And some are quite happy and successful. If you only know how to speak into discontent and crisis, you will miss most of your neighbors.

Most are spiritual. Most unchurched people believe in some kind of God. They're surprised and offended if you think of them as atheists.

They are not sure what "Christian" means. So you need to make that clear. You really can't make any assumptions about what people understand about the Christian faith. Moving forward, clarity is paramount.

You can't call them back to something they never knew. Old-school "revival" meant there was something to revive. Now that we are on the second to fifth generation of unchurched people, revival is less helpful, to say the least. You can't call them back to something they never knew. This should cause us to radically rethink our assumptions about ministry and culture.

Many have tried church, even a little, but left. At Connexus, where I serve, we have a good chunk of people who have never, ever been to church, but a surprising number of people have tried church at some point—as a kid or a young adult. Because it wasn't a good experience, they left. Remember that. It influences their biases and expectations.

They want you to be Christian. Unchurched people and people on the fringes of your church actually want you to follow Jesus authentically. Think about it: if you were going to convert to Buddhism, you would want to be an authentic Buddhist, not some watered-down version. Andy Stanley is 100 percent right when he says you don't alter the content of your services for unchurched people, but you should change the experience.[11]

They're intelligent, so speak to that. Don't speak down to people who are new. Just make it easy to get on the same page as people who have attended church for years by saying things like, "This passage is near the middle of the Bible." You can be inclusive without being condescending.

They hate hypocrisy. Enough said. Give it up. Change.

They love transparency. When you share your weaknesses, everyone relates (including Christians). People admire your strengths, but they identify with your weaknesses.

They invite their friends if they like what they're discovering. Ironically, new or infrequent attenders can become your best inviters if they love what you're doing. Because they are generally more plugged into the wider community than many Christians, it's easy for them to invite many friends to join them if at some point the gospel begins to resonate more deeply.

Their spiritual growth trajectory varies dramatically. One size does not fit all. You need a flexible on-ramp that allows people to hang in the shadows for a while as they make up their minds and one that allows multiple jumping-in points throughout the year.

Some want to be anonymous and some don't. Some unchurched people come in craving immediate connection and community. Others want to sit at the back, unnoticed, until they're ready to make a move. One size no longer fits all in greeting guests. Make your church friendly to both groups.

DEVELOPING A BETTER APPROACH TO INFREQUENT ATTENDERS AND UNCHURCHED PEOPLE

It's one thing to understand why people attend infrequently or stay away almost altogether, but it begs another question. How do you interact with them? What should your approach be when you connect with them?

By far, I believe the best response to infrequent attenders is simply this: you embrace them. I use the word *embrace* on purpose. There's something deep-seated in many of us that wants to reject people if we sense they're rejecting us. And people not coming to church much on Sunday can feel like rejection to an insecure church leader. (Which, by the way, is many of us on this side of heaven.) And unchurched people can initially seem so different in their attitudes, approaches, and even appearances from Christians who have been in the church all their lives.

In light of these dynamics, what do you do? You change your approach. What follows are different approaches and some new strategies that can help us bridge the gap as we move from a Christian era into a post-Christian era.

Show empathy.
Many of today's church leaders grew up in church. We remember a time when going to church was simply the thing you did every Sunday. And as church leaders or volunteers, it's what we *still* do every Sunday. So at times it can be a little hard to empathize with people who don't see things the way we see them.

Personally, I think participating in the mission of a great church weekly (including Sundays) is one of the best things a Christian can do. Unless I'm fooling myself, I think this is a personal conviction, not just a vocational conviction. If I stopped doing vocational ministry tomorrow, I would still want to participate weekly in the mission of a local church, including the Sunday ministry. But just because I see it that way doesn't mean everyone sees it that way. And here's the danger: if you start judging people for not seeing it your way, you will almost certainly turn them off. People—especially teens and young adults—can smell judgment a mile away. Judgment always creates barriers.

Empathizing with irregular attenders is not that hard to do if you realize you probably have an attitude about other organizations that mirrors their attitude toward your church. Take going to the gym, for example. I have a gym membership. Truthfully, as I write this chapter, I haven't been there in two and a half months. My attendance at the gym is less than stellar.

But my goal isn't actually attendance at the gym. My goal is fitness. So I spin on my bike trainer at home, do push-ups, and hike. I watch what I eat and I do other exercise. The gym is a means to an end, and it's not the only means for me. Am I going to make the cover of next month's *Muscle Magazine*? Well, they haven't called me yet. But that's not my goal.

Many people think the same way about church, especially unchurched people. If a formerly unchurched person shows up twelve times a year, that's far more than they've ever been in church! They might actually think they're doing great, and maybe they are, compared to how they used to feel and behave spiritually. So rather than judging them for it, tell them they're doing great. And invite them into a deeper conversation about faith and life.

I realize the gym analogy breaks down because I don't think the Christian faith is an individual pursuit like fitness can be (and clearly, I would be in better shape if I went to the gym three times a week and had a personal trainer). But if you stand there with a scowl on your face every Sunday, angry about empty seats, why would anyone want to sit in one? Showing empathy and compassion is a much superior strategy. It's also a much more Christian strategy.

Separate the mission from the method.

Somewhere along the way a lot of us end up confusing the mission and the method. Your mission is to lead people into a relationship with Jesus, not to get people to show up for an hour in a box every Sunday. Please hear me—I value our time together on Sundays as a church. And I think it's presently one of our very best vehicles through which to advance the mission of the church. But our mission is *not* to fill seats on a Sunday. It's to lead people to Jesus.

You should be obsessed with your mission, not with filling seats. But truthfully, some of us are more in love with the method than the mission. If that's you, repent. I have. I am.

That shift will create a whole new mind-set in your team. As Will Mancini has said, this attitude shift will help you run offense instead of defense on the issue of declining church attendance.[12] You'll start to think of fresh ways to help people on their journey toward Jesus.

And—don't miss this—if you really help people move into an authentic relationship with Jesus Christ, they might show up more regularly in your church on Sunday. Ironic, isn't it?

Celebrate wins.

It's strange that when children take their first steps, we applaud wildly, but when Christians take their first steps, we often look down on them or even dismiss them as immature. So new Christians don't read their Bible every day or attend every week or give the way you want. I get that. But many long-time Christians don't either.

Here's a deeper question: Rather than judging infrequent or new attenders, why not love them? Why not celebrate every time they take a step? Send a handwritten thank-you note to each first-time attender. Welcome them when they come back. Throw a party when they show up again three months later. Celebrate like crazy when someone gives their first five-dollar gift. Jump for joy when someone decides to serve, or high-five them when they decide to get in a group.

Okay, I'm exaggerating a bit. The point isn't to get weird. The point is to celebrate. As Andy Stanley says, what you celebrate gets repeated. Celebration is as much about attitude as it is about anything. And being someone who loves to work and loves to think, I don't naturally celebrate as well as others might. So who provides a good role model in terms of celebration?

Probably the best celebrator I know is Bob Goff. I don't

think I've ever met anyone with a bigger heart or who takes more delight in things others might ignore or despise. If you're really trying to figure out what Christian celebration looks like today, Bob's one of the best at it. Read his book. Stalk him (okay, don't stalk him, but do follow him).[13] Let some of his kingdom-of-God joy rub off on you. If the church approached ministry the way people like Bob approach life, the church would be a far more attractive and beautifully contagious group of people.

Elevate personal relationships.
While online relationships are real relationships, nothing is as powerful or meaningful as face-to-face connection. Facilitating a deep relationship is easier and more effective in person. Churches that value personal relationships (even for thousands of people through groups) will always attract people who value personal connection (which is, I think, almost all of us). A growing church that organizes everything around groups will always be more effective than a church that doesn't.

Love people.
Can you fully love people without being fully present? Do human relationships go to their deepest level in person? I think so. At least one in twenty couples who are married today began their relationship online.[14] But even those couples who meet online don't stay online—they get married. Love can be expressed online, but its fulfillment happens deepest through personal contact. Don't underestimate the

power in something as simple as love or grace. People crave it. The church in all of its forms is connected to the greatest source of love there is.

Create a culture of serving.

One of the problems with regular participation in online church is that it fosters a consumption mentality. You become the served, not the one who is serving.

Serving in church on a Sunday or in the community during the week is a chance to stretch and grow our faith. It reminds us that our faith is not about what we get, but really about what we give. When you get up early to set up portable church, lead a second-grade small group, greet people with a smile, work on the production team, or serve meals to the homeless, somehow you find a place in service of a goal greater than yourself. Make serving guests and others outside your community part of your culture.

Prioritize kids and teens.

Parents can catch a podcast or watch online, but kids really miss out when parents miss. To be with their friends who are running in the same direction and to have another voice (a small group leader) who knows their name, favorite food, and hopes and dreams saying the same thing a loving parent would say, is so far irreproducible in the online world. I believe that when the parents miss church, the kids are the biggest losers. The more you prioritize families, the more families will prioritize Sundays.

Create an irresistible experience.

The problem with many churches is that they're resistible. Our experiences aren't compelling enough to draw people back. Some of that is clearly related to us not loving people deeply enough or connecting people well enough relationally. And those should be among the things church leaders value most.

But there's also another element. Many churches don't value excellence. While there's an animated debate about whether churches should be "excellent," ask the question this way: Are we content with being mediocre? Framed that way, it's easy to see that a mediocre experience is a resistible experience. If your church is boring, why would anyone want to come back? You've already lost the battle.

Create an awesome online presence.

Even if people aren't with you, you can still be with them. A growing number of churches are offering online campuses. Interestingly, some are also shutting them down because online viewership competes too much with physical attendance. Your team will have to decide where it lands on that issue, of course. But you need to ask yourself whether the Internet is going away anytime soon. I think we all might agree the answer is no. So the question then becomes, how do we leverage it?

If your church doesn't have the budget or other resources to launch a full online campus, there are still many ways to develop an effective online presence. An effective social media presence is within the reach of any church. You have to know where your congregation lives online, and that varies depending on your community and the demographics near you. But between Facebook, Twitter, podcasts, a custom church app, your church website, and a church or personal blog, you have the opportunity to reach people every day wherever they are online. And none of those options costs much money or requires highly trained staff. Volunteers would be more than willing to help, and many are already great at social media and other online platforms because they do it for fun or for work. Each of these platforms can be a way to shape people's discipleship and even provide meaningful first contact or ongoing connection with unchurched people. Finally, giving to church online has never been easier. At Connexus, 70 percent or more of giving happens online. Other churches are seeing similar increases in online giving.

Church leaders today have an advantage that leaders simply didn't have a decade ago.

Social media and even e-mail are great ways to help people deepen their journey with Christ, not just push your latest program. What if you started viewing your social media channels and e-mail list as an opportunity to come alongside people and help them grow in their faith?

You have to be careful how you approach this, because if you're just trying to drive attendance, people will notice. But if you encourage them, inspire them, challenge them, and help them, they'll welcome your presence. If you run your social media and e-mail content through a *helpful* filter, people will be thrilled to hear from you. And it will deepen the bond you have with infrequent attenders. They'll come to see you as a friend, not just one more person trying to sell them something.

Be the favorite person in their inbox and their favorite thing to see on their news feed. Never underestimate what being helpful does for everyone involved.

Offer offline surprises.

If your Sunday experience is completely accessible online, mix things up a little at your physical location. Do something unique or fun in the parking lot, foyer, or service that you don't broadcast online. Create some memorable or poignant moments. Set up a photo booth in the foyer and let families get their picture taken for free when you're speaking on family. Celebrate a holiday together with a twist. For example, we gave butter tarts—a unique and amazing Canadian dessert—to every attender on Canada Day. They just happened to be made by the baker who was voted as making the best butter tarts in the country. We also make certain things, like branded coffee mugs and T-shirts (great gifts for attenders to hand to unchurched friends), available only on campus, not online. It creates a scarcity and rarity that makes people want to be there.

Start measuring outputs.

Will Mancini argues that church leaders are programmed to measure inputs, not outputs.[15] I agree. Typically, we measure how many people showed up, what they gave, who they brought, and even online traffic. But rarely do we measure outputs.

While measuring outputs will take some time to develop, it begins with a paradigm shift. What if the church became as much a sending organization as a receiving organization?

And along with that, what if you developed ways to gauge spiritual growth and the effectiveness of your witness to the community? Metrics could include how much time people spend with God personally each day reading Scripture and praying. The current statistics reveal a surprisingly low amount of personal Scripture reading and prayer among Christians. According to a recent study, 57 percent of Americans read their Bible four times a year or less. Only 26 percent read it more than four times a week.[16] What if you helped the people around your church change that?

And what if you got innovative and started thinking through whether people are better off five years after joining your church than they were before? Or whether they feel closer to Christ? Or whether they have a handful of truly deep friendships as a result of being associated with your church—the kind of friendship that allows 2 a.m. phone calls? Or what if you began to track whether people are impacting their workplaces and neighborhoods with the love and hope of Christ?

In other words, what if you helped your attenders *be* the church, not just *go* to church? What if you measured the impact of the sending as well as you measured the numbers associated with the gathering? Leaders get passionate about what they measure. So measure carefully.

Your Relevance Is at Stake

When things are changing this rapidly in the culture, it's critical that church leaders develop approaches that respond just as quickly. Any gap that emerges between the outdated methods of church leaders and the changing pace of culture produces one thing: irrelevance.

Rather than seeing this as an obstacle that's difficult to surmount, try to see this as an opportunity. The first-century church formed and spread rapidly in an environment that was more hostile to Christianity than the one the early twenty-first century offers.

Conversation #2

DISCUSSION QUESTIONS

Talk About It

1. Of the eleven reasons given for even committed church attenders attending less often, which are you seeing in your community and church?

2. To what extent has the trend of people attending church less often impacted your ministry over the last decade?

3. The characteristics of today's unchurched people are often indicative of a post-Christian generation. To what extent do they describe the people who live in your community?

4. What word best describes your church's attitude toward infrequent church attenders? Be honest.

5. Would you describe your church as being truly loving toward unchurched people? Why or why not?

6. Is your attitude toward infrequent attenders and unchurched people helping or hindering your mission?

Get Practical

Below are the eleven strategies we have discussed in this chapter to help you engage unfrequent church attenders and the unchurched. As a team, make notes on each approach, using these questions as a guide:

Which holds promise for you?

Which doesn't?

Which are you already doing?

Which seems completely foreign to you or too much of a stretch?

Which approaches would be easy for your church to adopt?

Which would be a challenge?

Which could you implement right away?

Which would take time?

1. Show empathy.
2. Separate the mission from the method.
3. Celebrate wins.
4. Elevate personal relationships.
5. Love people.
6. Create a culture of serving.
7. Prioritize kids and teens.
8. Create an irresistible experience.
9. Create an awesome online presence.
10. Offer offline surprises.
11. Start measuring outputs.

Make It Happen

Identify your single biggest obstacle to coming alongside infrequent church attenders and unchurched people. Once you've identified it, create a six-month plan to remove it.

In addition, identify two to five other key obstacles in your path. Now design a one- to two-year plan to address each of those obstacles.

Make sure you assign responsibilities and accountability and meet periodically to evaluate progress.

Conversation #3

ARE OUR LEADERS HEALTHY ... REALLY?

So far we've talked about creating organizationally and missionally healthy churches. But there's another aspect of health that gets overlooked far too often in the church, and that's the health of its leaders. The spiritual, emotional, relational, and physical health of a congregation's pastor(s) and leaders is a subject church leaders don't talk about nearly enough.

Here's the simple truth: healthy leaders create healthy churches. If a church's leadership is healthy at the top, that health will most often spread throughout the church. But the same is also true for unhealthy leaders and teams; eventually the entire body gets infected. The health of a congregation's leaders often determines the health of the congregation.

This conversation is significant because these days many leaders aren't healthy. I meet with a lot of church leaders in my traveling and speaking, and it's surprising to me how many admit (in one-on-one conversations) that they are not in a great place spiritually, emotionally, relationally, or physically. I say this not from a place of judgment but of empathy. I ran hard for a decade in church leadership, and our church grew rapidly. But I wasn't growing nearly as much on the inside as I should have been. In fact, on the inside I was crumbling in a few areas of my life.

After a decade in church leadership, I hit a wall. I burned out, moving through the darkest period of my life. It was as if I fell off a cliff and lost control of my heart, mind, energy, and strength. If you've ever been there, you know what it's like. And if you haven't, give thanks. For months, I could barely function. By the grace of God, I found a way to move through it, although full recovery took about five years. And even then, I didn't get back to normal; I had to find a new (and better) normal.

Health doesn't just happen in leadership. In fact, the demands of leadership will push you toward unhealth. The gravitational pull of leadership is away from wholeness. Headlines seem to offer a revolving door of athletes, politicians, preachers, and business leaders who have to step back because of a moral failure or scandal. Not surprisingly, under every scandal is an unhealthy leader. If you add to that the number who leave leadership for "personal reasons" (often a polite way of saying they're simply done, burned out), the body count is huge. I'm incredibly thankful that my collapse didn't take me to a place of infidelity or moral failure. I didn't even buy a sports car or quit my job. But for a season I thought it would take me out of ministry.

HOW TO TELL IF A LEADER IS BURNING OUT

So how do you know you're burning out as a leader? How do you know whether you're unhealthy? Following are nine things I personally experienced as I burned out. While you should consult with your doctor or a medical professional if you believe you might be suffering from burnout or depression, these signs have alerted many that they're burning out. A combination of several of them might indicate that indeed you're far beyond just tired.

1. Your motivation is fading.

One sign of burnout is that the passion that once fueled you is gone. This impacts your drive as you discover that the source of your motivation has vaporized. Alternately, your motivation may not be entirely gone, but it might have shifted—from being focused on the mission to being focused on yourself. Pain, after all, is selfish. Drop a brick on your toe and see if you can think of anything other than the pain. A shift toward a self-centered motivation is a danger sign that there is pain in your life that needs to be addressed. It's interfering with your ability to lead passionately and well.

2. Your main emotion is numbness.

You no longer feel the highs or the lows. This was actually one of the earliest signs for me that the edge was near. I said to my wife that it felt as if my heart went dead. I just couldn't feel what I was supposed to feel anymore.

3. People drain you.

Of course there are draining people on the best of days. But not everybody, all the time. Burnout often means few to no people energize you anymore. You want to be alone. And while solitude is a gift from God, isolation isn't.

4. Little things make you disproportionately angry.
When you start losing your cool over small things, it's a sign something deeper is very wrong. Disproportionate emotions of any sort are often a sign something is awry.

You're becoming cynical.
Many leaders fight this one, but cynicism rarely finds a home in a healthy heart.[17]

Your productivity is dropping.
You might be working long hours, but you're producing little of value. Or what used to take you five minutes just took you forty-five. That's a warning bell.

You're self-medicating.
You usually either practice self-care as a leader or you end up self-medicating. I'll spend a little more time on this symptom because it's so widespread. When you think of self-medication, don't just think of pills or alcohol. As you'll see below, there are some very socially acceptable ways even for Christians to self-medicate. But the results are still numbing.

Overeating. Being overweight or even obese is almost normal in some Christian circles. As someone who has to watch my weight carefully (and who does not understand how anyone can be a natural beanpole), I empathize. That said, food is the drug of choice for many Christian leaders.

Working more. Again, working too many hours is socially acceptable, even rewardable in some circles. As a recovering workaholic, I know. But all work and no play doesn't just make you dull; it makes you disobedient. It's ironic, but the way some leaders cope with the stress associated with work is by working more. It numbs the pain.

Gossip. It's just a theory, but I think when we feel bad about ourselves, we say bad things about other people. Often church leaders who have failed to care for themselves end up with enough toxins inside that they want to take down others.

Spending. Whether it's retail therapy at the mall, ordering more of your favorite pursuit online, or the constant climb into a bigger house, a better car, the latest tech, or the latest trend, Christians can easily numb their pain by endlessly accumulating things that end up in a landfill one day.

Under-the-radar substance abuse. Sure, you're probably not going to develop a cocaine addiction. But sometimes it can be more subtle than that. Whether it's a drink every day when you get home or an overuse or misuse of your legitimate prescription, Christian leaders can fall into the classic pattern of turning to a substance rather than turning to God for relief.

5. You don't laugh anymore.
Nothing seems fun or funny, and, at its worst, you begin to resent people who enjoy life. Misery loves company.

Sleep and time off no longer refuel you.
Sometimes you're not burned out; you're just tired. A good night's sleep or a week or two off will help most healthy people bounce back with fresh energy. But you could have a month off when you're burned out and not feel any difference. I took three weeks off during my summer of burnout, and I felt worse at the end than when I started. Not being refueled when you take time off is a major warning sign you're burning out.

Those are not the only signs, but they are signs many people experience. Again, if you suspect you are burning out or are burned out, I would encourage you to seek immediate professional help—a medical doctor and a trained Christian counselor. Maybe you think it's just a season and you'll push through it. That worked for me ... until it didn't work anymore.

BURNOUT DOESN'T DISCRIMINATE: PERRY NOBLE'S STORY

As I indicated, many church leaders struggle with burnout. That even includes successful, well-known leaders like Perry Noble. Perry wrote an incredibly honest book about his burnout and depression called *Overwhelmed*, and I had the chance to interview him on my leadership podcast. Perry was exceptionally raw and real with me about how bad it got and how desperately he wanted to end his life, even while leading New Spring Church in Anderson, South Carolina, one of the fastest-growing churches in America. He told an amazing story of how he overcame anxiety and depression to keep leading.[18]

Perry summed up the danger of burnout really well when he told me, "Carey, I really seriously contemplated suicide on more than one occasion. It's just one of those places. I had a friend say this: 'It's kind of like eating at Denny's. Nobody goes there intentionally, but you just kind of wind up there sometimes.' That's what happened to me. If you would have asked me when I started, 'Hey, what's your goal in leadership?' I would not have said, 'I want to get to the place where one day I want to take my life.' But I got there, and it happened over a period of time."

The Culprit: Unhealthy Patterns

A number of factors led Perry to depression, anxiety, and the brink of suicide. To begin with, he said he never rested. As his church grew, the criticism got to him, but instead of dealing with his pain, he buried it in more work. He said, "One of the most unhealthy patterns for leaders is that we'll get into a season where maybe things are growing, or things are going well ... During that season, we rev up our engines so much that we never take a day off. We never take a day of rest."

Perry so rightly pointed out that overwork is the most rewarded addiction in our culture. People praise you for working hard, and the praise feels good. "They will sing your praises right up until you get into your coffin, and then, they'll forget about you," Perry said. "We can get so addicted to positive things said about us, it can push us into thinking,

'Oh my gosh, the world can't live without me. I can't rest.'" Overwork combined with success can eventually lead to an adrenaline rush addiction. Like most workaholics, Perry stopped making time to have fun, even though he had a young family and a great team around him.

Looking back, he said he saw the irony that you're often more creative when you're having fun and taking time off than when you're not: "There are times when you get relaxed, when you get in an environment where you start having fun, and you have the best ideas. ... So what if we, as leaders ... took one day a week and just did something fun that we enjoyed? A fully charged leader can accomplish more than a partially charged leader, every time."

Recovery

What turned it around for Perry? It was taking the exceptionally painful step of admitting his struggle to those close to him. He had lots of shame about it, even more than he'd experienced when he had a pornography addiction years before. But when he confessed to his best friend, the heaviness lifted. "A lot of people have been forgiven for their sin, but they've never been healed because they've never confessed it. There's a big difference between being forgiven and being healed," Perry pointed out. "I learned the power of being healed by confessing that out loud and just telling somebody, 'Hey, I'm wrestling.' Because I told him, I was able to tell my leadership team. I was able to find a good Christian counselor who was able to walk me through some things and navigate me through some things."

Finally, Perry also realized that his anxiety and depression required medication. "If something's wrong with the brain, medically, there's a chemical imbalance in the brain. If God, through common grace, has given us science and medicine to be able to fix that problem, then we shouldn't just try to pray that problem away. If God has given us medicine to try to heal that problem, then I think we should take it."

Over to You

I hope you realize that if you're struggling, you're not alone. Pride will push you to think you can handle anything. Fear will keep you from telling anyone you can't. Despite Perry's story (or my story), if you feel there's still too much of a stigma attached to burnout, anxiety, and even depression to feel comfortable talking about it, get over it. Once you crash, you will have no choice but to tell people. If you start the dialogue early, you might be able to get help early and prevent a full-out crash.

The only way you will ever last in ministry over the long haul is to stay spiritually, emotionally, physically, and mentally healthy.

TEN HEALTHY OPTIONS FOR SELF-CARE

So maybe you're not burned out, just in a tough season. We all get there. How do you stay healthy? How do you go from surviving to thriving? The best thing you can do as a leader is take excellent care of yourself. When you carve out time to take care of yourself, you'll always be in a better position to take care of others. A church leadership team composed of healthy individuals has a much better chance of becoming a truly healthy team. Ironically, it's in caring for others that most leaders make the mistake of neglecting self-care.

That said, staying emotionally, spiritually, relationally, and physically healthy is easy to understand but takes discipline to realize in your life. While there may be nothing truly novel in these ten options, when you practice them they have a staggeringly positive impact on your personal health and well-being.

1. A great daily time with God:
Whatever method you use, time with God matters.[19] And your personal walk with God is often a casualty of ministry. Why is that? It shouldn't be! Personally, I read through the Bible every year. I find it helps me tackle passages I'm not preaching on and reminds me that I'm a follower of Jesus first and a leader second.

2. Exercise:
Being out of shape physically means you will never be in top shape mentally or emotionally. I don't like exercise either, but I kept at it until I discovered a form of exercise I liked. A few years ago, I discovered I like cycling and I invested in a road bike. Your story will be different. You might end up

walking, hiking, running, taking up CrossFit, or competing in marathons. It's up to you. The point is to get moving.

3. A healthy diet:

You are what you eat. We're learning daily how broken the food chain is and how closely our physical and mental health is tied to what we eat. Dumping the processed foods for whole foods can be a great place to start.

4. Proper sleep:

In some circles it's seen as cool to brag about how little sleep you get. But not with healthy leaders. Get seven to eight hours a night. Take naps. I really think sleep is one of the most underrated leadership secret weapons there is.[20]

5. Intentional white space in your calendar:

Most leaders are afraid to make appointments with themselves or even to budget time for message writing, planning, or thinking. You can schedule appointments with yourself, time off, and downtime in the same way you schedule meetings. Just do it![21]

6. Healthy friendships:

Ministry can be draining. When was the last time you hung out with a friend you didn't need to minister to? Who makes you laugh until you cry? Go hang out with them. Regular doses of life-giving relationships can make such a difference.

7. Margin:
You are at your most kind when you have the most margin. Ever notice that? I find that's true of me. It's true in terms of my calendar but also true of finances. How can anyone be generous with their heart, time, money, and attitude if they have nothing left to give?

8. Hobbies:
Writing, blogging, and podcasting are my hobbies these days. You can be much more interesting than that. Take some pictures. Take up hiking. Get crafty. Study the constellations. Your hobby will fuel some passion in your life.

9. Family time:
Take a road trip. Go out for dinner. Have some fun! Throw a ball in the backyard. Play hockey in the driveway or shoot hoops.

10. Coaching and counseling:
For about twelve years I've had coaches and counselors who have helped me get through road bumps and life issues. They have been invaluable. Yes, I pay them money, but it's an investment in my family, my church, and my life. I'm different and better for it.

I know at the end of your life, you will be so much better for pursuing the path of self-care rather than the path of self-medication. Self-care takes intentional planning, but it's so worth it. Eventually leaders who don't care for themselves end up out of leadership or ineffective in it.

YOU'RE NOT ALONE

So how healthy are you? How healthy is your team? I realize those are exceptionally personal questions. I also realize the answer can precipitate a life crisis. But if you're burning out, the crisis is coming anyway. You might as well get in front of it. And if you're only moderately unhealthy, dealing with it is still by far the best option. You can get back to normal, but it will be a new normal.

As a team or church board, it's important to create a healthy climate in which people can be honest about how they're *really* doing. At first the conversation might seem shocking or even overwhelming. Hang in there. The way you hold this conversation will be pivotal. Create a safe place for people to talk without fear of judgment. Offer to help anyone and everyone who needs help.

After all, remember the mission is at stake. One of the best gifts you can give your church is a healthy set of leaders. Actually, it's the best gift you can give their spouses and their kids as well. So do whatever it takes to have an honest conversation about health. And then get healthy.

And to every leader reading this who realizes they might be burning out … you're not alone. You're really not.

DISCUSSION QUESTIONS

This conversation will be a little more difficult than the others in this book because the subject is inherently personal. If you have someone on your team or in leadership who you suspect is burning out, it might be a good idea to have a one-on-one conversation with them rather than singling them out in a group or dropping "hints" in a meeting.

Nonetheless, teams are wise to talk about burnout as a way of ensuring they stay healthy. Please realize that the group questions, though, are no substitute for well-motivated, loving, and honest conversations that happen one-on-one.

Talk About It

1. Have you been in an organization where a leader has burned out? What was it like?

2. Did anything in my story or Perry Noble's story about burnout surprise you?

3. Is the health of your leaders a goal your church actively pursues?

4. What could you do to ensure your leaders stay healthy?

5. *Workaholism is the most rewarded addiction in our country.* To what extent does your church culture reward workaholism?

6. Of the different ways that leaders self-medicate, which are most prevalent in your church?

Get Practical

1. Does your church have a network of trusted Christian counselors to whom you can refer your leaders and members? If not, what will you do to put one in place?

2. In addition to checking in on leadership issues with staff and key volunteers, many healthy churches will also check in with leaders on a personal level. What do you need to do to create the kind of culture in which these conversations can happen regularly?

Make It Happen

Is there anyone on your team who is showing more than a few signs of burnout? Are they aware they might be burning out? What will you do to help them?

WHAT KEEPS HIGH-CAPACITY LEADERS FROM ENGAGING OUR MISSION?

Where would your church be without volunteers? It's a bit of a scary question, isn't it? Inherently, churches are volunteer organizations. Practically, churches cannot run simply on paid staff. The model is unfeasible, and the work is simply too great. But it's more than just a practical reality; it's a theological necessity, too. God has given people gifts and talents that are designed not just to glorify Him but also to help the church accomplish its mission. So for both theological and practical reasons, the church will always be a volunteer organization with, at best, a limited number of paid staff who equip and lead volunteers in fulfilling the mission of the church.

So, with that in mind, how are your volunteers doing? Too often, churches settle for a mediocre volunteer culture. Realizing that the faithful will always serve, leaders fail to be intentional about the experience they create for volunteers. A suboptimal culture is inevitably the result. Ask most volunteers how well supported, encouraged, and nourished they feel, and they'll tell you they feel overworked, undervalued, and undersupported, even if they love their church and the leaders under whom they serve.

Because of a mediocre culture, most churches retain just enough volunteers to keep things afloat. This also has a serious and unintended consequence—higher-capacity leaders stay away. They simply don't want to be a part of poorly led teams. The result is that church leaders can't find enough great leaders who

> can attract other capable leaders;
>
> don't drop balls;
>
> love a challenge;
>
> constantly overperform.

And yet the very people who attract other capable leaders, don't drop balls, love a challenge, and regularly overperform stay away from the team because of how it's led.

In many cases, the very leaders you're hoping to attract are in your congregation; it's just they won't serve until you change the culture. The conversation in this chapter focuses on how to do just that. It's a critical conversation because engaging your best leaders and volunteers will take your mission to a whole new level. It simply will.

THE QUESTIONS EVERY VOLUNTEER ASKS BUT NEVER SAYS OUT LOUD

So what's your culture really like? Sometimes it's hard to drill down deep enough to find the truth. Honest conversations are hard to come by. But if you try hard enough, you can imagine what they'd sound like. One way to get honest feedback is to poll your volunteers. But my guess is that—particularly in the church—your volunteers might be too polite to tell you exactly how their experience has been. Go ahead and ask (it won't hurt), but take it a step further.

So what's the next step? Ask the questions you would ask if you were a potential volunteer. Every volunteer asks questions about an organization, even if they never say them out loud. How do I know? The same way you know. I've asked the same questions myself when I've signed up to serve somewhere. My guess is you have as well. The team that understands this has a distinct advantage in attracting and keeping great volunteers. Leaders who get this can create the kind of culture in which volunteers thrive.

Develop great, healthy answers to these five questions, and volunteers are far more likely to stick around. Better yet, they're likely to grow and flourish under your leadership.

1. Are the relationships around here healthy?

No community should have better relationships than the local church. After all, our faith is based on a Savior who reconciled the world to Himself, forgiving our sin. What could we possibly hold against one another? And yet often the local church is home to some of the most fractious, passive-aggressive relationships out there. We have a Savior who came full of grace and truth, yet church leaders will often swing to either extreme: all grace, so issues are never dealt with, or all truth, so people get hurt. Many people love the mission of the organization they work for; they just can't stand the personal politics and dysfunction.

One of the greatest gifts church leadership can give to a congregation is healthy relationships. So be healthy. We talked about personal health extensively in chapter 3. But the basis of health in an organization, other than having healthy leaders, rests on changing one thing. Talk *to* people you disagree with, not *about* them. That will change far more than you think.

2. Will serving help me grow spiritually?

It's ironic that in many churches and organizations, people equate serving with burning out, not being renewed. And yet Christian service should be a paradox of renewal: When we give our lives away, we find them. When we serve, we grow.

Growth flourishes in a healthy environment. Pay attention to the issues addressed by the other four questions, and you'll have an environment that favors growth. But you also need to care for volunteers spiritually, or at least provide an environment in which spiritual growth flourishes. This goes along with giving them personal attention.

Pray for them.

Pray with them.

Share your journey.

Encourage theirs.

Mentor your key leaders.

You can't guarantee spiritual growth will happen, but you can provide the environment in which it can easily happen.

3. Am I just a means to an end?

I wish I could get some of my early years of leadership back. As much as I would have denied it at the time, I think I naturally saw people as a means to an end. The end was (and is) a great one: fulfilling the mission of Christ's church. But people matter. A lot. Nobody likes feeling used, but that's often how churches and other organizations treat people.

The answer here is similar to that of question 2. Care about them. Encourage them. Ask questions. Listen to their stories. Pray for them. When you have a healthy, Christ-centered, energized team that knows they're valued, the mission advances further and faster anyway.

4. Will you help me develop the skills I need?

A friend of mine who has visited a lot of churches and non-profits recently told me that—as well-intentioned as leaders are—the vast majority of organizations are, in his view, poorly run. That's a tragedy.

Why is the local Walmart better run than the local church? Seriously. One is selling products that last a day, a month, or a year. The other is brokering life change that lasts forever. The church should be the best in the world at recruiting, training, and releasing people into ministry and their calling.

Many volunteers who come your way are highly capable people who just need a little training to know how to master the specific task you're giving them. A good heart just needs to be supplemented with a good skill set. Set aside an evening or a Saturday to properly train volunteers as they start serving, and then top up their training from time to time to help them get better at what they do. Don't just leave them to figure out what to do all by themselves.

5. So, am I signing up for life?
In many churches, serving is like the Hotel California. You can check out any time you like, but you can never leave. You're a Christian for life, but that doesn't mean you have to serve in one role for life. But many churches just assume people will.

What if you start putting a time line on every role? What if your conversation sounded more like: "Why don't you try this for a season? Can you serve with us for this semester/year?" Or say something like, "People in this position typically serve for a two-year term. You can try it out for a month before you commit to that term."

Every church will definitely have some longer-term serving positions (for example, at Connexus, we ask our high school small-group leader to serve for four years, but we're clear on the term from the outset). Most other roles can easily be shortened to a few months to a year.

If you start providing end dates for roles and create a healthy volunteer culture, you'll notice something surprising. Many people stay after their term has ended. They'll actually sign up for more. Surprisingly, when you give volunteers an out, many lean in. At Elevation Church in Charlotte, North

Carolina, for example, volunteers are interviewed every six months and can elect to keep serving or stop. It facilitates some incredibly healthy conversations, according to family ministry director Frank Bealer. (For more on Elevation's innovative approach to volunteers, listen to episode 20 of my leadership podcast.)

REASONS HIGH-CAPACITY PEOPLE LEAVE YOUR TEAM

Answering the questions above is a great starting point to creating a healthy volunteer culture. But there are other factors that take a team from functioning to outstanding. And again, many church leaders miss these. If you pay attention to them, your volunteers can begin to thrive. In fact, some volunteers might tell you that your church provides the best environment in which they've served, period—their workplace included. If you think about it, why shouldn't the church offer a better environment in which to work and serve than most businesses? Why can't the church be the most rewarding place to serve?

To keep your highest-capacity volunteers engaged, you have to be hyperintentional about your volunteer culture. If you fail to keep high-capacity leaders engaged in your church mission, it's likely because of one of these factors.

The Challenge Isn't Big Enough
People with significant leadership gifting respond best to significant challenges. Underchallenge them and they won't stay

engaged for long. So many church staff and nonprofit staff I talk to are worried about giving their volunteers too much responsibility. Surprisingly, that might be exactly why you *don't* have enough high-capacity volunteers. The best leaders want a meaningful challenge. If you're underchallenging them, they'll leave. How do you overcome this? Give your biggest challenges to your best leaders. Check in on them and support them, of course, but don't shy away from giving capable people big challenges.

Your Vision, Mission, and Strategy Are Fuzzy

People want to serve a cause bigger than themselves. Which is great, because that's what the church, and even most nonprofits, is all about: causes bigger than themselves. But often our mission, vision, and strategy are fuzzy. Mission is the *what*. Vision is the *why*. Strategy is the *how*. Even if they're written on a piece of paper, in many organizations most people functionally can't tell you what they are. That's a shame. The motivation for volunteers *is* the vision. Their fuel is the *why* behind the *what*. And—get this—the church has the best vision and mission on planet Earth. So why on earth do we hide it?

Without clear vision, volunteering ends up being about filling a slot, meeting a need, or doing your duty. Or, in the worst case, volunteering can become more about serving the ego of the leader than it is about serving Christ. But when you keep the true mission of the church or your organization central, people rally. For example, in addition to leading a local church, I sit on the board of directors for an extremely well run local food bank. Their mission? *A city in which no one is hungry.* That's inspiring. Give your volunteers something to focus their hearts on, and they will give you their time and energy.

You're Disorganized

Disorganization is epidemic among church leaders and non-profits. Few things are more demotivating than giving up your time as a volunteer only to discover the staff person responsible didn't set you up to succeed. The tools they need to do the job are missing or incomplete. The rest of the team is late. Or maybe—worse—they're not even 100 percent sure what they are supposed to do or how they are supposed to do it. You can always find people who will put up with disorganization, but many more will simply give up. And high-capacity people will make a beeline for the door. The more organized you are (on time, prepared, other holes plugged), the more your volunteers will be able to excel at what you've asked them to do

You Let People Off the Hook Too Easily

I know, I know. They're *volunteers*. And you can't hold a volunteer accountable, can you? Yes. You most certainly can. And should. For everyone's sake. If a volunteer is late, it's really no different than if a staff member is late. Sure, you want to address it kindly, but you need to address it.

Again, few things are more disheartening for a motivated volunteer than if they did their homework and showed up early only to find that others didn't, and then, to top it all off, a staff person excuses the behavior of the people who didn't pull their weight with lines like, "It's okay; we're just glad you're here." The high-capacity leader dies a thousand deaths every time he or she hears a staff person utter those words. And then, almost 100 percent of the time, the organized, highly motivated, exactly-the-kind-of-leader-you-were-hoping-to-keep volunteer will leave, and the slackers will stay.

You're Not Giving Them Enough Personal Attention

Another big challenge for church leaders and nonprofit staff is the innate desire most of us have to treat all people "equally." You don't want to play favorites, so everyone should be treated the same. Again, that's a mistake.

The church should *always* be a loving organization. But certain people require more of your time and attention. Unless you're intentional, you'll end up spending most of your time with your most problematic people and the least amount of time with your highest-performing people. Flip that. Cut ties with the low performers and spend most of your time walking alongside and developing your best leaders. And before you think that's completely unfair, just know your entire team will thank you for it because you'll end up with a strong team.

By the way, Jesus did this, too. He had crowds of disciples, but then a group of seventy-two, an inner group of twelve, an inner circle of three, and he placed his greatest investment in one (Peter).

You Don't Have Enough Other High-Capacity Volunteers Around Them

It's never fun to lead alone. As soon as you find a high-capacity volunteer, your next step should be to recruit more and move others alongside them. Nurture this team. Build into them. Take them to lunch. Take them with you when you travel. Do life with them (again, I think Jesus modeled this pattern). Like attracts like. And the more high-capacity leaders you have serving, the more you'll likely attract.

Sadly, many leaders don't do this, and high-capacity leaders once again walk away, demotivated.

Treat Volunteers the Way You Want to Be Treated

If you think about it, creating a great volunteer culture is closely tied to the Golden Rule: treat others the way you want to be treated. Create the kind of organization in which *you* would like to serve.

By being organized, holding people accountable, keeping the mission front and center, and employing some of the other strategies outlined in this chapter, you'll create the kind of culture in which people love to serve. It's worth your time and effort, because in churches and the nonprofit world, leading and managing volunteers is one of the most important tasks you'll have. Quite literally, the mission depends on it.

DISCUSSION QUESTIONS

Talk About It

1. Have you ever asked any of the five questions volunteers ask but never say out loud? Which questions do you ask most frequently?

2. How healthy would you say your volunteer culture is on a scale of 1 to 10, with 1 being very unhealthy and 10 being extremely healthy? Discuss the reasons for your answer.

3. Do you think your church currently does a good job engaging high-capacity volunteers? Why or why not?

4. Is the sense of challenge at your church high enough to attract high-capacity people? What could you do to challenge people at a higher level?

5. What do you think would happen to your mission if your volunteer culture became significantly healthier? What could you accomplish that you're currently not accomplishing?

Get Practical

1. Would your volunteers describe your staff or senior leadership as well organized? What impact do you think

your level of organization/disorganization is having on your volunteers?

2. Discuss creating end dates on the terms of service for your volunteers. With which teams could you start this practice? Remember that when you give your volunteers an out (and have a healthy culture), many lean in.

3. Do an honest analysis of your training and ongoing support for your volunteers. Do you do a *great* job of preparing and supporting volunteers? If not, what will it take you to do a better job in these areas?

Make It Happen
Identify your single biggest obstacle to creating a great culture for volunteers. Once you've identified it, create a six-month plan to remove it.

In addition, identify two to five other key obstacles to creating a great volunteer culture. Now design a one- to two-year plan to address each of the obstacles.

Make sure you assign responsibilities and accountability and meet periodically to evaluate progress.

WHY ARE YOUNG ADULTS WALKING AWAY FROM CHURCH?

We've talked about how our culture is changing rapidly. Not only are most churches not growing and people who attend church attending less often, but of the Christians who are leaving the church, none are leaving more quickly than millennials—young adults under the age of thirty.

In this chapter, we'll drill down even further into the mass exodus from the church that we're witnessing. Unlike chapters 1 and 2, this is not about people we're failing to attract; it's about people who once attended and have left. Specifically, younger people who grew up in the church and are walking away from church and/or faith.

We'll look at some research on the issue of why teens and young adults are leaving, and then we'll explore why a model of church (attractional church) that has been very effective for several decades may indeed be reaching the end of its exponential growth curve. In all of this, we'll discuss why people who have tasted and seen ... are leaving.

GETTING FAITH TO STICK IN KIDS AND TEENS

So why are kids and teens walking away from the faith they grew up in by the time they're young adults? I realize this subject is heartbreaking because we know the kids and young adults who are walking away. We raised them. They may even be your kids. If you're reading this book, there's little question you *want* kids to follow Christ. And naturally, you want *your* kids to follow Christ. Yet the staggering truth is that 40 to 50 percent of students who are active in the church in their senior year of high school will drift away from the church as young adults. Did you catch that? Not 40 to 50 percent of kids, but 40 to 50 percent of kids who are active in their final year of high school will walk away. Why?

Fortunately, when it comes to kids, we have research. Kara Powell, PhD, is a mom, a youth ministry veteran, and the executive director of the Fuller Youth Institute. I had her on my leadership podcast to talk about her decade-long research project that sheds light—and hope—on this growing problem for parents and church leaders.[22] The results are published in her *Sticky Faith* book series.[23]

Kara's team has studied youth group graduates, families, and more than 150 churches in an effort to find out how to reverse the trend of young people drifting from the faith. Her research has covered different denominations, different-sized churches, and different regions. While she didn't find a silver bullet, she did find certain behaviors in youth that related to mature faith, which in turn seems to predict how well young adults "stick" with church. Her findings are nuanced and varied, but here are a few of the highlights.

Forming Intergenerational Relationships

Surprisingly, one of the key factors in developing a faith that sticks is intergenerational ministry and relationships. As Kara explained, "[For years], we put our children in one part of the building, we put our youth across the parking lot or in another wing of the building, and the adults are someplace else. As a result, high school students graduate and they know youth group, but they don't know the church." If age-specific environments are the only experiences churches offer, students grow up spiritually and relationally impoverished.

The solution isn't to revert automatically to intergenerational worship that attempts to span all age brackets and, in the process, ends up speaking to no one well (it's exceedingly difficult to communicate to eight-year-olds, twelve-year-olds, and forty-three-year-olds at the same time). So how do you provide multigenerational experiences? Different ages need to develop relationships with one another. The older need to mentor the younger. Churches can offer this through multigenerational groups, with teens in community with older group leaders, or even by mixing up college-aged students with empty-nester adults as leaders or group members. Many millennials are looking for spiritual parents, and these groups and mentor relationships can provide that.

Perhaps the most effective way to partner the generations is through serving. Pairing a teen or child who's volunteering with an adult can be a fantastic way to grow and learn together, provided the adult realizes there's a mentoring opportunity and responsibility that comes with it. If the adult simply sees the younger volunteer as an extra set of hands or "help," the opportunity will be lost. But the environment of doing ministry together *with* a younger adult, child, or teen can be exceptionally formative for both the adult and the younger person.

Giving and Receiving Grace

The *Sticky Faith* research also demonstrates that churches that show grace to teens do better than churches that don't. Kara pointed out that kids grow up in youth group hearing lists of what they should and shouldn't do. "When we fail to live up to that checklist, then young people end up running from God and the church, just when they need both the most," she said. "And here is what young people need to understand, and adults, too, is that … once we fail, the same grace allows us to go back and receive forgiveness and restoration from God and through the faith community. So grace is not only what enables us to obey; it's also what enables us [to live in community] even in the midst of our ongoing failure."

All of this raises a bigger question. How transparent should parents be with their kids about their own struggles? The *Sticky Faith* research suggests parents could foster more authentic dialogue by opening up with their children and being honest about some of their own mistakes, whether those mistakes were made in the past or even more recently. Even if it's just apologizing for losing it in the moment, being open and saying you make mistakes can go a long way in creating a meaningful dialogue. The honesty can start when your kids are young, too. "It is never too early to start implementing some of these principles and to make your home a safe place to talk about mistakes," Kara said.

It's also never too early to have faith conversations with your kids and talk to them about your own faith. Many parents are afraid to open up out of fear they're not far enough along in their own faith journey to lead their kids. Kara noted, "Our research isn't saying you need to be more spiritual than you already are; our research is saying to share with your kids the spirituality you already have." The fact that they see the faith you have trumps any worry about them seeing any faith you don't (yet) have.

Expressing Doubt Safely

Perhaps the biggest surprise in the *Sticky Faith* research is the role of doubt in a young person's faith journey. It's natural and perhaps even logical to think that doubt is fatal to faith, but that's not what the study found at all. Kara explained: "Our research shows that it's not doubt that is toxic to faith—it is unexpressed doubt that is toxic to young people's faith." In many ways, that's exactly the kind of research churches need to help kids, teens, and young adults move forward in their faith. Everyone has doubts. But few of us (even adults) feel safe discussing them. What if the church became exactly the kind of place in which people felt safe expressing their doubts? Kara says that the church has to become a forum in which deep doubt and big questions can be safely expressed: "Do young people feel like they can ask big and tough questions about God in our community? And if not, how can we create more safe places so that they can? So if you know a young person whose big questions about God are causing them to drift from their faith, then I would say, how do you make sure they stay in the conversation? Whether it's in small group, whether that's in ongoing one-on-one mentoring with an adult at your church ... because if we don't provide venues for conversation to happen, then they're going to have conversations in other places and come to conclusions we wish they wouldn't come to."

The evidence strongly suggests that churches that create safe, nonjudgmental, personal, and authentic forums for dialogue are going to see more of their kids stick than churches that don't. Add to that some intergenerational mentoring and shared experiences, and the odds of a child's faith sticking as he or she gets older increase.

WHY MANY MILLENNIALS HAVE STOPPED ATTENDING CHURCH

The Barna Group has done a particularly good job of tracking the attitudes of both churched and unchurched millennials toward the church. A 2014 study cited (among others) five compelling reasons church engagement and attendance continue to decline among millennials.[24] Of course, the good news is that once you spot the trends, you can work at reversing them.

While the following assessment of the church's culture might seem harsh (once again), as it is with confession, the truth can and will set you free.

1. The church is irrelevant, the leaders are hypocritical, and leaders have experienced too much moral failure.

Sure, that's three reasons in one. But the research lists all three reasons together, and millennials arguably see them as such. This bears itself out in actual conversation as well. Talk to unchurched people about why they don't go to church, and, quite predictably, you will hear them rattle off a list of objections that is almost certain to include their beliefs that the church is irrelevant and full of hypocrisy. After all, just look at the moral failure of so many of its leaders.

To some extent, you can't blame people for this perception. You and I both wince every time we see another headline announcing a new moral failure. And far too many Christians have been burned by the judgment of the perpetually self-righteous who live within our churches.

If you want to attract and keep millennials, it's critical that you foster a culture of integrity, authenticity, and grace. Jesus said that it would be by our fruit that people would recognize us. Live a life of integrity with each other and outsiders, and your church will become a magnet for people searching for God, both for younger adults and, I think, for many others. That kind of integrity and grace is far too rare in the world, let alone in the church.

2. God is missing in the church.

Millennials who engage the church are actually looking for God, but too often they feel as if their search is in vain. It's ironic, but a growing number of people claim to be going to church looking for God but say they are having difficulty finding Him. It may hurt to admit that this could be happening within your ministry, and you might even discount the few who would make this accusation, but in an age where perception is reality, this criticism is too pointed to ignore.

The paucity of personal experience people say they have with God in many churches is disturbing. It would be easy to point at rock-show churches and blame them (I lead one of those—I'll deal with the issues in those kinds of churches later in this chapter), but the truth is that people in all kinds of experiences, from liturgical to charismatic, have left the church in search of God. Although some would disagree with me here, I'm not sure leaving the church for an individualized, personal, or even home-based experience of church helps people find God any better. In fact, I think a meaningful percentage of people who leave the church in search of God find themselves further away from God five years down the road than they'd care to admit, but that isn't stopping people from leaving. In our consumer-driven culture that applauds individually tailored experiences, what if the real paucity is that we have lost a sense of what true maturity and the experience of God is?

Regardless, the accusation still stings and must be taken seriously. Are people who are coming to your church looking for God actually finding him? If not, why not?

3. Legitimate doubt is prohibited.

Millennials will often have the courage to say out loud what our teenagers are reluctant to express. And in this case, what's driving teens away is what's also driving or keeping millennials away: the perception that doubt can't be honestly expressed. Truthfully, I empathize with people who levy this criticism at the church today. It is very difficult to have an honest conversation in many churches, both conservative and liberal. In many conservative churches, legitimate questions get dismissed with pat—and often trite—answers. In many liberal churches, there is often so much ambiguity that questions that actually *can* be answered are left unresolved—as if leaders are taking people nowhere. Church leaders simply have to get better with handling the tension that comes with questions.

So how do you do apologetics? Or is that a dying art? At Connexus, I recently taught a nine-part series called "Skeptics Wanted" in which we invited people to ask their toughest questions about Christianity.[25] I gathered people's questions through an online survey and then systematically addressed them. But rather than present "slam dunk" arguments that dismissed the critics and skeptics, I tried to take their claims seriously, engaging them as worthy objections. Of course, I presented strong evidence for why the Christian faith makes sense, but I also wanted to engage the seriousness of people's questions. Above all, the series was designed to be an invitation into a deeper dialogue. Not only did it spawn great discussion of honest doubt in small groups, but we ended it with an invitation to have a coffee on us at Starbucks for anyone who wanted to talk further, well aware that even a nine-part series wasn't going to settle things once and for all in every person's mind. Instead, it would be one step on a longer journey. I think this kind of conversational environment will become crucial in future churches.

4. People aren't learning about God.

It's one thing to attend church and find God missing; it's another to attend church only to find God present but incomprehensible. It still strikes me as incredible that people come to church seeking God only to leave not understanding anything they hear. One couple that attends our church told me that they tried to go back to church when their kids were young only to give up in frustration after a year. The reason? They couldn't understand anything the pastor taught. The woman said, "It was like he was speaking a foreign language." After five more years out of the local church, they decided to give it one more shot when they came to our church. I'm so grateful they were willing to try again.

The truth is, you and I can relate. Every one of us has listened to a sermon for forty-five minutes only to walk out the door tremendously unclear about what was just said. And—preachers—come on: we've all *given* more than one of those messages.

The solution is simple, yet so many people miss it: clarity. Speak in everyday language, not in churchspeak or in a meandering way. It takes far more work to be clear than it does to be confusing. And no, being clear is not the same as dumbing down a message. You can be thoughtful without being confusing. But it does take great intentionality and preparation to have a clear point to your message. It's also vital for preachers and communicators to be clear about what they want to happen in people's lives when people leave.[26]

5. They're not finding community.
The Barna study points out that despite a growing epidemic of loneliness, only 10 percent report going to church to find community. Sometimes I wonder if it's because people expect the church to be the last place they'll find community. And that's tragic.

Of the many criticisms that can be levied at the church, lack of community shouldn't be one. *Nobody should be able to out-community the local church.* You can make a legitimate argument that one of the reasons behind the explosive growth of the first-century church was because of the way they loved each other and the world. Love should be a defining characteristic of the local church. If we loved the way Jesus loved, people would line up out the door.

As your church grows larger, small groups become essential. For us at Connexus, *everyone* has a place in a group— from preschoolers right through to seniors. No matter how big or awesome the weekends might be (and they can be awesome), small group is where life change happens most deeply. Among many other strategies for reaching and keeping families, elevating community is an approach we've learned from Orange. If you want more, cultivating an excellent small-group strategy is outlined in *Creating a Lead Small Culture* by Reggie Joiner, Kristen Ivy, and Elle Campbell, and in *Lead Small* by Reggie Joiner and Tom Shefchunas.[27]

Personally, I'm grateful for research that helps us discover how people in a rapidly changing culture actually feel about the church. It can only help us get better at being the church as Christ called us to be.

COOL ISN'T ENOUGH (ANYMORE)

A final word on how to stop people from walking away from your church. For the last few decades, simply being a cooler church than the church down the road helped churches grow. There was a day when all you had to do was *improve* the church you led in order to gain traction. Trade in the choir for a band. Turn the chancel into a platform. Add some lights, some sound, some haze. Get some great teaching in the room. And voilà—you had a growing church. People stuck around. People dug in. And new people joined.

We're quickly moving into a season where having a cool church is like having the best choir in town: it's wonderful for the handful of people who still listen to choral music. And irrelevant to everyone else. Something's changing. Many leaders think that moving a pulpit out and replacing it with a stage and adding lights and a good video system might move them from stagnation to growth overnight. They'd be wrong. If there was ever a time when that alone would grow a church, that time has recently come to a close. Sometimes all a good video system does is magnify your irrelevance. Hundreds of thousands of dollars in lights and great sound gear are probably not going to impact your community like they used to.

You might think I'm against churches having bands, lights, and creating a great environment. Not at all. In fact, the church I lead has all of the above; if you are going to gather people, gather well. My point is not that you *shouldn't*. My point is that it's no longer *enough*. And maybe it never was.

The megachurches many of us watch today didn't get to be as effective as they are simply by being cool. If you really study how most large churches have become effective in leading people to Jesus (and, yes—doubters, suspend judgment— many large churches *are* effective in leading people into a real relationship with Jesus Christ), they have always been about more than just lights, sound, and show. There's substance. More substance than critics would ever give them credit for.

Are megachurches universally healthy? No. But neither are many small churches. In fact, sometimes the dysfunction in small churches eclipses that of medium-sized or large churches. So why would cool church be fading into the sunset?

Cool Church Isn't What It Used to Be

Decades ago as cool church started to take root among large, rapidly growing churches, many other, smaller churches and church plants followed suit. And for a season, it "worked." Getting some awesome lights, better sound, better music, and a slightly more hip communicator grew churches. Sure, some of the growth was transfer growth, but a large percentage of what many churches experienced was not transfer growth. People invited their friends and their friends came back.

So what's changing?

To begin with, most cities now have a great selection of cool churches. Many towns have at least one. It's no longer unusual to have a band in church. It's not even that novel to have lights and great sound or to play all the cool songs. And in the process of all this imitation, three things have happened.

Cutting-edge keeps changing ... fast. Constant connectivity online has sped up trends, memes, and the spread of information. What's novel isn't novel for long anymore. You used to have to hire experts, be in a certain circle, or do some travelling or sleuthing to find cool things. Now you just download an app, watch a video, stream a song, or follow whatever trend you're passionate about in the moment—whenever you want to. Instantly. Usually for free. Consequently, there's kind of a trend fatigue or indifference happening. Trends are shorter, less interesting, and we're all growing oh-so-bored with what's novel. Which means that it's harder than ever for churches to be cutting-edge because cutting-edge keeps changing.

Indifference to church has grown. As the percentage of unchurched adults in the United States has risen from 30 percent to 43 percent of the population, indifference to the church has grown.[28] Church leaders in places like Canada, Europe, Australia, and New Zealand have felt the indifference for much longer. As churches changed their worship style and even architecture in the '80s, '90s, and 2000s, having a cool church got you more traction than it does today. And yet as indifference grows, it's having less and less of an impact. Here's why: if people aren't into church, it doesn't matter how cool, hip, or trendy your church is; people won't be that interested. You understand this pattern from other areas of your life. If you're on a health kick, for example, you're not going to order the burger and fries, even if they are the best in town. If you're not on a health kick, the spinach, arugula, and kale salad with tuna isn't going to capture your imagination, no matter how healthy or on trend it is.

Imitation killed innovation. Because we live in a digital age when church leaders easily keep their fingers on the pulse of what other leading churches are doing, we also find ourselves living in an age of imitation. I'm not against borrowing great practices from other churches or leaders. There can be an arrogance to a leader who feels as if he or she has to reinvent the wheel each time they face a situation, or who is simply too proud to learn from others. But with access to trends, imitation has a shadow side.

To begin with, when churches imitate each other, we rarely borrow all the best practices. We rarely borrow all the best practices. We just borrow the ones that seem obvious or perhaps have caught our imagination. Often the imitation is just that—imitation, not the studied adaptation of a nuanced model. Too many times we're looking for silver bullets, tricks, or gimmicks that will move our church into a growth phase. All the while we ignore the reality that what's making growing churches grow is significantly deeper than the cool factor. Consequently, leaders who finally get what they were longing for—a cool church—are often shocked to discover they don't deliver what they promised. And in the process of all that imitation, something even more important is lost: innovation.

What's needed now more than ever is church leaders willing to pioneer, to go deep into a culture that keeps changing to reach people who are increasingly resistant. What's needed most as we look at what's ahead is innovation. And it's sorely lacking among many church leaders. It is even more difficult to study your culture prayerfully along with the best practices of other churches and then burrow deep into something that perhaps no one has tried before in an attempt to advance your mission It is even more difficult to prayerfully study your culture along with the best practices of other churches and then burrow deep into something that perhaps no one has tried before in an attempt to advance your mission. But the future will require more leaders and teams to do exactly that. Wise leaders won't let imitation kill innovation at their church.

Is Cool a Bad Thing, Then?
So should you run from all things cool, trendy, or hip? No. The answer to the challenge of keeping up with relevance is not to return to irrelevance. Relevant church has many critics, but *not* bridging the cultural gap is even more dangerous (in my view) than trying to bridge it and maybe failing. All around us is a rapidly changing culture, and when we ignore that culture, we do so at our peril. It is still a great idea to use the culture to reach the culture. So what do we do as we head into the future?

Five Keys to Rebirth (The New Cool)

The church can take many forms. For all those leaders who, like me, believe in gathering people together for the sake of a larger mission, I think you stay relevant (and, yes, a bit of cool is always in order), but you definitely go beyond that. Dig deeper. Here are five keys I see to a future of greater impact with millennials.

1. Authentic Leadership and Connection

Sometimes the reason cool doesn't connect is because underneath all that "cool" is an inauthenticity: people who are uncomfortable with themselves, trying to compensate for something, or who have somehow fallen for the lie that style trumps substance. Again, that may have worked at one point or it might still work in some contexts, but that won't be true for much longer. Unchurched people and younger adults and teens are looking for authentic leadership and authentic connection. Quite simply, authentic resonates. More than ever, people are looking for what's real, what's true, and what's authentic.[29] And, my goodness, if the church is anything, it should be a place of deep authenticity.

2. An Elevated Sense of Mission

The church has always been about something bigger than itself. At the center of our mission is Christ. While most organizations naturally drift toward an insider focus, church leaders must resist this at all costs. Not only is it antithetical to the true mission of the church, but a self-obsessed community is a turnoff to a young generation that is well aware of the needs in the world the church often ignores. You lose your narcissism when you lose yourself in a bigger mission. And a bigger mission, by the way, is something millennials are longing to give their lives to. A church that is focused on a larger mission will never become self-obsessed.

3. Hope

We leaders are dealers in hope. And Christianity provides more hope than anything. I'm 100 percent behind making messages practical, applicable, and helpful. I think the gospel is that.

But sometimes the practical can tip too far. We recently heard from an unchurched woman in her mid-20s who had listened to a few of our messages and said, "Well, it's great to know how to balance my personal finances … but I don't really need God for that, do I?" To some extent, she's right.

The gospel is practical, but it is much more than that—it is supernatural. Christianity at its best has always been about both imminence and transcendence. As millennials and young adults explore the Christian faith, there has to be practical theology, but there also has to be much more.

4. Elevated Community

I'm all for video walls if they help the mission, but as my friend Reggie Joiner says, the church will never be able to out-Disney Disney.[30] That's very true. No church will ever have the budget or resources to entertain or engage better than Disney or Hollywood. But even if the church did, what would be the point?

While we can't out-Disney Disney, no one should be able to out-community the local church. God is in the people business. And the heart of Christianity is relationship—a right relationship with God, with each other, and with ourselves. It's also fairly clear that younger adults and teens hunger for community perhaps more deeply than previous generations did. Moving forward, churches that elevate community and prioritize healthy intentional relationships will fare much better in accomplishing their mission than those who don't.

5. Experimentation

How's your church at experimentation? When you talk to many leaders, you realize that the words *experimentation* and *church* do not easily fit together in many circles. Experimentation, of course, is the key to innovation. And, as we've seen, in an age of imitation in the church, innovation has to make a comeback. So how does a church experiment? Particularly a church that has had success in the recent past or even in the present?

The best approach (if your church is moderately effective in accomplishing its mission) is to do what you do now, but begin experimenting on the side to see what has the potential to make a significant impact in the future. Truthfully, I'm not sure anyone really knows what that is right now. Which is why experimentation is even more important than we might initially think.

HOPE IS RIGHT AROUND THE CORNER

I realize that having conversations like the one anticipated by this chapter and chapters 1 and 2 can at times feel over-whelming or even moderately depressing. I hope your team doesn't end up at that point. The goal is not for us to feel overwhelmed but to see the opportunity.

As Jim Collins has shown us, a significant component in effectiveness as a church or organization is the willingness to confront the brutal facts.[31] Church teams that do this—look honestly at the changing culture and at themselves—have a distinct advantage over churches that don't. The first step in getting healthy or staying effective over the long run is a willingness to have the conversations few others are willing to have.

While you already know this, hope springs from honest conversation. The truth truly does set you free.

Conversation #5

DISCUSSION QUESTIONS

Talk About It

1. Would you say that kids walking away from their faith in their teen or young adult years is an issue in your church? To what extent? How do you know?

2. If teens and young adults have expressed reasons why they're walking away, what are they? Make a list.

3. Is your church a safe church in which a person can express doubt about what they believe? Why or why not?

4. Do you have any environments in your church in which adults can interact alongside kids and teens in a meaningful way (beyond being their Sunday school teacher or group leader)?

5. If a millennial were to walk into your church, how would he or she find God? Or would that visitor say God is missing in your church?

6. In this chapter, we saw that cool isn't enough anymore. Of the five keys to the rebirth of "cool church," which would you say accurately describe your church? Where do you have the greatest work to do?

Get Practical

1. Convene a focus group of teens or young adults who are walking away from your church or who have walked away from your church, maybe over dinner or coffee. Ask them why they're making the decision to walk away, and then don't judge; just listen. Listen and take notes. Discuss what you've learned with your team afterward.

2. Create a plan to intentionally pair adults with kids and teens so they can serve together. Prepare those adults to do more than simply "use" the kids and teens as extra hands. Prepare the adults to become mentors to those kids.

3. Do a serious assessment of how well your church is prepared to handle conversations with those who doubt, both formally and informally. Talk to your group leaders or Bible study leaders about allowing people to express their doubt without others rushing to quick or easy answers.

Make It Happen

Identify the single biggest reason kids are walking away from your church as teens or young adults. Once you've identified it, create a six-month plan to remove it.

In addition, identify two to five other key obstacles that are driving teens and young adults away. Now design a one- to two-year plan to address each of the obstacles.

WHAT CULTURAL TRENDS ARE WE MISSING?

The rapid shift in culture has been a refrain throughout this book so far. That's because the shift happening in our culture is, I think, seismic. Historians still speak of the radical changes that happened to Western culture (and beyond) when, more than seventeen hundred years ago, the Roman Emperor Constantine made Christianity the official state religion of the empire. In my view, the shift happening now in the West toward a post-Christian culture will be something equally dramatic. And naturally, as people caught in the midst of a cultural shift this size, we are unable to understand all the implications and consequences, in the same way fourth-century Christians who grew up being persecuted couldn't have understood what happened to their culture as Christianity took hold of the Roman world and beyond. Our vision is partial, and the change continues to evolve beyond our control.

That doesn't mean we can't know anything about the shifting culture. While conversations like this will always be temporary in nature and subject to change, it's imperative to have them. If you're over forty (and many church leaders are), the world into which you were born no longer exists. And if you're trying to reach people younger than you, your assumptions about what they value, what's happening in their lives, and how they see the world will often be inaccurate. Church leaders who study the trends happening around us and stay current with shifts in thinking and ideologies will always have an easier time connecting with emerging generations than those who don't.

And yet this is a conversation that's easier *not* to have than it is to have. When you lead an organization—especially when you are responsible for leading an organization like the local church—there is a temptation to ignore trends or minimize the impact they will have on how you operate. This is particularly true in successful churches. If it's "working," why bother to think about the day when it might not work anymore? Add to that the fact that it's so difficult to gain momentum that, when you have some momentum, it becomes tempting to ignore the changes around you because they might force you to rethink your method. But the truth is that your method (your strategy, your approach, your plan) is not sacred; the mission is sacred.

Churches that will thrive over the long run will study culture, and in that process, they will become flexible, agile, and adaptive. In a business context, Andy Molinsky calls this characteristic of certain leaders and organizations "global dexterity": the ability to adapt behaviors across cultures without losing who you are in the process.[32] Leaders who are willing to reconsider the methods to preserve the mission are usually the ones who succeed long term.

To that end, new and emerging trends are all around us.

You can't miss them, actually. Our lives are impacted by them every day. *Yet many church leaders are not talking about their impact.* I suspect one of the reasons we're not talking about these issues might be that few of these trends have clear-cut or obvious implications for the church; there are no easy or snappy answers. Most of the thinking around these trends leads to what I call "wet-cement conversations": thoughts that are open to reshaping, rethinking, and reconsidering. Not every leader is comfortable with that kind of conversation. But what follows are many of the issues that we indeed need to be thinking through, observing, and praying over. Even if it results in speculative conversations for your team, to speculate is better than to ignore. And, naturally, you will add your own opinions and observations to the dialogue as it develops. It's exciting to think of what might happen if thousands of church leaders engage the realities that continue to unfold around us in Western culture. Church leaders who see the future can seize the future.

CULTURAL TRENDS CHURCH LEADERS CAN'T IGNORE (BUT MIGHT)

While there are dozens of trends impacting the culture, the trends that follow are what I would call "organizational sleepers." These are the ones that, at least in my view, church leaders are most likely to ignore when gathered around a leadership table.

Online as the new default. Less than two decades ago, you had to *go* to church to hear a message or to experience church music. Or you had to ask someone to mail you a cassette or CD of the service. In other words, it was work. Now you just need a smartphone. Every attender can (and often will) listen to any communicator, band, or concert they want. And almost everyone who shows up at your door has checked out your church online before they came. *What are you doing to embrace the online world beyond a barely supported and moderately outdated website, podcast, or Facebook page?* (The conversation about online being the new default is explored in greater detail in chapter 2.)

WiFi and smartphones. On that note, WiFi is everywhere, and even if it's not publicly available in your church, people still have their phones. People who are listening to you are Googling you while you're speaking. When you make your announcements and invite them to something, they're checking out other options while you're listing yours. *Do you assume your audience is intelligent, literate, and has options?*

Dialogue. People want to talk, not just listen. While sitting around tables every Sunday may not be the answer, increasingly a church without conversation is a church without converts. Churches that elevate community across the ages, from kids to adults, will have a more effective ministry than churches that don't. *What scalable, meaningful venues do you have for people to visit online and in-house for real conversation?*

Loyalty. Brand loyalty is low. Four of the top five global companies didn't exist forty years ago.[33] Being around for a long time can be seen as a liability with the next generation.[34] And even if you are a church plant, loyalty is still fickle. *How are you showing the relevance of an ancient faith to the current generation?*

Lack of guilt. Guilt used to motivate people to change and even to come to faith. The next generation feels less guilt than almost any previous generation. In many church circles, loyalty is earned, in part, by making people feel guilty if they don't serve, don't give, or leave. This simply becomes less effective with every passing year. *Are you still using guilt to motivate people?*

Declining trust in authority. People will still trust authority when the authority has *earned* their confidence. But most people today, particularly unchurched people, start out with suspicion as their primary approach to the church and its leaders. More than ever, trust is earned slowly and lost instantly. Authentic, honest, transparent leadership will continue to be far more effective than closed, secretive, or powertrip-style leadership. *Is the way you exercise authority worthy of people's confidence?*

Declining trust in institutions. The generation that had inherent trust in institutions is disappearing. Today, leaders have to show people how an organization can help them, because by default, they don't think it can or will. Most people will opt for self-directed spirituality over institutionally led spirituality (see the next point). *How are you demonstrating trustworthiness?*

Personalized, eclectic spirituality. People want to find their own unique path, and most start out that way, exploring different faiths and even making up their own versions of what they think faith should be. Eventually, some of them will embrace the path of Christ, but they don't start out there. *How do you embrace where they start but encourage them not to finish there?*

Desire for greater purpose. As noted in other chapters of this book, millennials will not stay long at work or causes that have little greater meaning or purpose. They have no desire to help any leader preserve an institution or tradition; instead they want to be part of a mission that is accomplishing something significant in the world. Younger leaders, by the way, get this, which is why you need them in your organization.[35] *Are your mission and vision clear, compelling, and inexhaustible?*

Personal mission. People aren't waiting for some organization or leader to change the world—they'll just do it themselves. From charity runs to starting nonprofits from home, the next generation not only believes they can have a global impact— many are having it. If your church doesn't have a burning sense of purpose and vision, you look lame compared to the average twenty-two-year-old. *How is your vision motivating people who have vision?*

Trust in user reviews. What you say about your organization matters less than what others say. People place far more trust in user reviews than in advertising copy. On sites like Amazon, the user reviews are read with much greater care than any copy produced by a publisher or manufacturer. *What are others saying about your church, and how would people find that out?*

The death of cash and checks. When was the last time you wrote a check or paid $500 cash for something? No one does that anymore. But every Sunday most church leaders expect most of the offering to come in via cash or check. *Is most of your giving happening online? Why not?*

Those are twelve microtrends in our culture that deserve the attention of church leaders, and you can come up with many more. I'll outline a few more in this next section specifically related to technology and the way people consume content, and then I'll take a (dangerous) crack at answering the most perplexing questions of all: Where is all of this heading? What will the future church be like?

FIVE THINGS NETFLIX IS SHOWING CHURCH LEADERS ABOUT THE FUTURE

Netflix and other on-demand video providers have already changed the culture more than you think. And they've probably changed *you* more than you think. It feels like a long time ago that people gathered around a TV screen together to watch a show live when it was first broadcast. The way we view and consume content as a culture likely has massive impact on the way the church will interact with people in the future in terms of distributing and sharing content (messages, Bible studies, kids' curriculum, and more). There are at least five ways the changes introduced by Netflix (and the like) will impact the future church.

1. Live, simultaneous viewing is dying.

About the only thing many people watch live now is sports, particularly if you monitor the viewing habits of people under forty. Even regular shows people follow are often DVR'd so people can skip through commercials. Even though I'm over forty, I rarely watch network television; but when I do, I'll record a show and start watching it fifteen to twenty minutes late so I can skip the commercials. A couple of implications for church leaders:

> *Will once on Sunday seem strange?* People are increasingly used to listening to your content on their schedule. If your main draw on Sunday morning is the message, offering it only once live on Sunday will not resonate as much in the future as it has in the past. While this might not mean adding more services (extra services with twelve people attending are not compelling), it does force you to reconsider what you're doing and why you're doing it.

Relationships and mission will be more powerful than singing and speaking. While a message and music have always been important aspects of Christian gatherings, the gathering of the church at its best has always been about more than just a service or even a message on Sunday. The church is a community on a common mission in which relationships with insiders and outsiders are central. Churches that elevate relationship, both for new attenders and regular attenders, will see far more effectiveness in the future than churches that don't. In fact, you might even see more people drawn to your church not just for the services but also for the relationships and for a chance to make a difference working together on a common mission. If all you do is sing and speak on Sunday, it will become harder and harder to gather a crowd.

2. Watching is becoming personal, individual, and portable.

Like you, I now consume content on multiple devices. I can watch TV, movies, and Netflix on my phone, iPad, laptop, desktop, or TV. And, like you, I simply pick up where I left off. Stop a show at 33:23 on one device and pick up at 33:24 on another, whenever you want. Start at the gym and finish in the car or on the back deck.

Netflix allows subscribers to create individual users on a common account so your kids or spouse can watch what they're watching and you can watch what you're watching without messing up each other's feed. As a result, various members of a household may be watching the same series but will be at different places in the series.

The implication for church leaders is that one more shift from the communal to the individual is happening. And that tears at the fabric of what the church is about—a community. So what on earth does that mean?

It's an opportunity for people to access your content the same way they access other content. Like many churches, we created an app for Connexus that allows people to stream messages whenever and wherever they want across devices. Our content is available on our website in addition to via podcast. Accessing your messages will become more personal, individual, and portable. Embrace it. I realize that this sometimes means people will watch online rather than attend, but it's also a great way to spread the message more quickly than otherwise. People who love what you do will share it with their friends and talk about it on social media.

People will still need to feel connected to something greater. As people's experience of content consumption on an individual level becomes more prevalent, the need for community still won't go away. We're more connected than ever as a culture, and many people are lonelier than ever. As much as people want individualized access to content, they also want to be part of something bigger than themselves.

Mission-driven, mission-focused, and relationally rich churches will draw in people longing for something bigger and more significant than themselves.

3. There's a market for binge watching.

Binge watching is increasingly normal. Although it may have started back in the '80s or '90s when people lined up VCR tapes or DVDs and watched them in a marathon session, now it's just far too easy to press *play* from your couch without ever getting up. Since Netflix streams entire series commercial free, you can easily power through several seasons of your favorite show in a week or even a day. New seasons of series are now released all at once rather than episode by episode (week after week) as in the past, again resulting in binge watching for many viewers.

The implications for church leaders are actually quite good on this one. People will consume really great content in marathons, including yours. Your audio podcast could become a place where people go through an entire series while on their commute or working out. Your video podcast could become the subject of binge viewing. Ditto with your website. Some churches like North Point are even building microsites around each sermon series.[36] Bottom line? Make sure your content is accessible in the *easiest* forms possible for people to access.

4. Great stories are alive and valued.

It's becoming widely accepted that the best content being produced these days is not coming from Hollywood or even network TV, but from cable specialty channels and new content producers, like Netflix itself. Those shows win the ratings wars because of rich plot lines, complex characters, and willingness to take viewers seriously. Many of these cable series refuse to dumb down their content. Many critics believe TV has become what movies used to be: a forum in which great stories are told.

The gospel has always been about God's story intersecting with the human story. The church is uniquely positioned to tell the best story of all. So do it, *well*. Clearly people are looking for a better, richer, deeper story. Church leaders need to bring it to them.

5. People will pay for something they don't use, until one day, they won't.

I realize I pay almost $100 a month for something I almost never use: network TV. I rarely watch it anymore. I hold out and pay the monthly bill because I *might* watch the World Series or the Super Bowl. I don't do illegal downloads, and watching live sports in Canada legally without subscription TV is more difficult than in the United States. But seriously—$1,200 a year in case I *might* watch something? I could almost fly to the World Series for that.

For the first time in the United States, traditional television subscriptions are declining.[37] This is only going to accelerate. If your entire church model is built on people coming together at set times to "consume" content, how long will it be until people eventually wake up and realize they are paying for something they rarely "use"? This is a bit of hyperbole, of course, when it comes to the church, because the church is *so* much more than a common gathering around content. Except that sometimes it's not. It should be, but it's not.

If you are simply trying to attract people to a one-hour event that people increasingly don't attend, you will always struggle. People will support something they don't attend until one day, they won't.

The good news? Mission-centered, mission-focused churches will not be impacted by this. A church that has a white hot sense of mission will almost always have the resources it needs to do what the church is called to do. But churches who want to prop up what used to sort of work won't. So focus on your mission. Focus on your purpose. Call people to something greater than themselves.

WHAT WILL THE FUTURE CHURCH LOOK LIKE?

So if everything's changing, what will the church look like in the future? That's a great question, and the truth is, no one is 100 percent certain. While no one's *really* sure of what's ahead, talking about it at least allows us to position our churches for impact in a changing world. So, borne out of a love for the gathered church, here are a few thoughts. Consider it thinking in pencil, not ink.

Gatherings will be smaller and larger at the same time. While many might think the megachurch is dead, it's not.[38] There are more people attending large churches than ever before, and that trend continues to accelerate. We will likely see large churches get larger. The multisite model will continue to explode as churches that are effective expand their mission. At the same time, churches will also establish smaller, more intimate gatherings, as millennials and others seek tighter connections and groups.[39] Paradoxically, future large churches will likely become large not because they necessarily gather thousands in one space, but because they gather thousands through dozens of smaller gatherings under some form of shared leadership. Some of those gatherings might be as simple as coffee shop and even home venues under a simple structure. We will see the emergence of bigger churches and smaller churches at the same time as the gathered church continues to change.

Churches will have a quicker, lighter footprint. Ancillary to the trend of churches becoming larger and smaller at the same time, growing churches will adapt a quicker, lighter footprint—a phrase I learned from Rich Birch.[40] Many large churches have expanded over the last decade by erecting large campuses that cost millions of dollars to build. That may continue in select cases, but for most churches, if you're waiting for millions to build your building, you might wait forever. Churches will get innovative and start looking at portable and nontraditional ways of growing ministry.

Quicker, lighter footprints will be necessary as the economics of church change and the agility needed by churches to respond to growth continues to escalate.

They will prioritize a for-you *not a* from-you *culture.* Andy Stanley often talks about what he wants *for* people, not just what he wants *from* them. Churches in decline often think in terms of what they can get *from* people—money, time, growth, etc. Churches that will make an impact on the future will be passionate about what they want *for* people—financial balance, generosity, the joy of serving, healthier families, and of course, Christ at the center of everyone's life.

More church staff will come from the marketplace rather than seminaries. This breaks my heart, but the most gifted leaders are not flocking toward ministry or seminary anymore (I wish they would). They are heading into the marketplace. The best church staff moving forward will not be products of traditional seminaries. Sure, there will be exceptions, but for the most part, you will assemble your team from gifted and passionate people who already attend your church and have never thought about ministry as a vocation. (You might end up sending some of them to seminary after the fact.) I realize this trend has been happening for several decades now in growing churches. But I think in the next decade this will hit the senior pastor position harder than ever. Maybe the senior pastors who will lead the best churches of the next twenty years won't come from seminary. How we will get them educated in Scripture and theology remains a question. Rethinking theological education is critical.

Churches that love their model more than the mission will die. Many individual congregations and some entire denominations won't survive the next ten years. The difference between those who make it and those who don't will be the difference between those who cling to the mission and those who cling to the model. When you go through a cultural shift as deep as the present shift, the mission survives but the model changes.

Think about the invention of the car. When the automobile was invented, it quickly took over from the horse and buggy. Buggy manufacturers were relegated to boutique status and many went under, but human transportation actually exploded. Suddenly average people could travel at a level they never could before. The mission is travel. The model is a buggy, or car, or motorcycle, or jet.

Look at the changes in the publishing, music, and even photography industry in the last few years and you'll see the trend. The mission is reading. It's music. It's photography. The model always shifts, moving from things like eight-tracks, cassettes, and CDs to MP3s and now streaming audio and video. Companies that show innovation around the mission (Apple, Samsung) will always beat companies that remain devoted to the method (Kodak).

Churches need to stay focused on the mission (leading people into a growing relationship with Jesus) and be exceptionally innovative in their model.

The church will still gather. As radical as the shift we're seeing is, the church will continue to gather on weekends. If you read the comments on a sampling of church leadership blogs, you might think that some Christians believe the best thing to do is to give up on Christian gatherings of any kind. This line of thinking is naive. While some will leave, it does not change the fact that the church has *always* gathered because the church is inherently communal. What Christians can do together far surpasses what we can do alone. So while our gatherings might shift and look different from they do today, they will endure. They might even spread and grow.

Consumer Christianity will die and a more selfless discipleship will emerge. Consumer Christianity asks, *What can I get from God?* It asks, *What's in it for me?* That leads us to evaluate our church, our faith, our experience, and each other according to our preferences and whims. Many critics of the church have left under the pull of consumer Christianity because "nothing" meets their needs.

All of this is antithetical to the gospel, which calls us to die to ourselves—to lose ourselves for the sake of Christ. As the church reformats and repents, a more authentic, more selfless church will emerge. Sure, we will still have to make decisions about music, gathering times, and even some distinctions about what we believe, but the tone will be different. When you're no longer focused on yourself and your viewpoint, a new tone emerges.

Sundays will become more about what we give than what we get. The death of consumer Christianity will also change how we gather. Our gatherings will become less about us, our preferences, and our tastes, and more about Jesus and the world He loves. Rather than a gathering of the already convinced, churches that remain will be decidedly outsider focused. And words will be supplemented with deeds.

In the future church, being right will be less important than doing right. Sure, that involves social justice and meeting physical needs, but it also involves treating people with kindness and compassion in everyday life and attending to their spiritual well-being. This is the kind of outward focus that drove the rapid expansion of the first-century church.

Attendance will no longer drive engagement; engagement will drive attendance. Currently, many churches try to get people to attend, hoping it drives engagement. In the future that will flip. The engaged will attend, in large measure because only the engaged will remain. If you really think about this, engagement-driven attendance is exactly what has fuelled the church at its best moments throughout history. It's an exciting shift. As we saw in chapter 2, ironically, leaders who value attendance over engagement will see declining attendance.

Simplified ministries will complement people's lives, not compete with people's lives. For years, the assumption has been that the more a church grew, the more activity it would offer. The challenge, of course, is that church can easily end up burning people out. In some cases, people end up with no life except church life. Some churches offer so many programs for families that families don't even have a chance to be families. The church at its best has always equipped people to live out their faith in the world. But you have to be *in* the world to influence the world. Churches that focus their energies on the few things the *church* can uniquely do best will emerge as the most effective churches moving forward. Simplified churches will complement people's witness, not compete with people's witness.

Online church will supplement the journey but not become the journey. Online church and social media have shown up at many points within the discussions in this book. So what will happen to it years down the road? I think in certain niches, online church might become the church for some who simply have no other access to church. But there is something about human relationship that requires presence. Because the church at its fullest will always gather, online church will supplement the journey. I believe that online relationships are real relationships, but they are not the greatest relationships people can have. Think of it like meeting someone online. You can have a fantastic relationship. But if you fall in love, you ultimately want to meet and spend your life together. So it is with Jesus, people, and the church.

Online church will become more of a front door than a back door. A second truth about online church is that its audience will likely change within the next five to ten years. There's no question that today online church has become a back door for Christians who are done with attending church or only feel like attending in person on occasion. While online church is an amazing supplement for people who can't get to a service, it's still an off-ramp for Christians whose commitment to faith is perhaps less than it might have been at an earlier point.

Within a few years, the dust will settle and a new role for online church and online ministry will emerge. Online church has the potential to become a massive front door for the curious, the unconvinced, and for those who want to know what Christianity is all about.

In the same way you purchase almost nothing without reading online reviews or rarely visit a restaurant without checking it out online first, a church's online presence will be a first home for people and, for many, will lead to a personal connection with Christ and ultimately the gathered church.

Online relationships will be valued as real relationships. Churches that haven't ventured much beyond a website are going to miss the boat. Real interaction with real people online is, well, real. Sure, face-to-face is deeper, but people will tell you things online they can't muster the courage to tell you face-to-face. Whether you get them to a "real" church is increasingly debatable. I would love that. But we'll have to see. As much as you might hate it, virtual relationships are becoming real relationships.

THE FUTURE IS GOD'S … AND YOURS

Ultimately, I have a lot of hope for the future church. I hope you do, too. The mission is too important to think otherwise. The church has withstood much over the centuries, and because it is Jesus' idea, not ours, the church will endure. That said, the church is a unique divine-human partnership; God could have chosen to act alone. Instead, he chose to partner with us to reach the world with his love. So your response as a leadership team really matters. As more and more church leaders pour their hearts, minds, and souls into the challenges and opportunities ahead—and share what they learn with other leaders—we will see the mission of the church become effective for a new generation.

DISCUSSION QUESTIONS

Talk About It

1. How has the world you grew up in changed? Which changes do you like the most? Which do you like the least?

2. As you read through the twelve trends listed on pages 113–117, which surprise you the most?

3. Which of the twelve trends has your church addressed? Which trend appears to be the one you are least ready to deal with?

4. How have you seen the content consumption patterns created by companies like Netflix influence the way people interact with your church?

5. Are Sundays at your church more about what people get or more about what people give? In what ways is that distinction important?

6. Of the eleven predictions about what the church will look like in the future, which are you most ready to embrace? Which are you least ready to embrace? Why?

7. Does what's happening with online church and social media feel more like a threat to you or an opportunity to you? Why?

8. What do you think will happen to your church if you ignore these trends?

Get Practical
So much is changing in our culture, it's hard to know where to start. Re-read the chapter and select between two and five trends that you think you are best prepared to respond to. Which is most prevalent in your area? Which is most prevalent in the age group you're trying to reach?

Make It Happen
Identify the single best opportunity you have to respond to a cultural trend that's impacting your ministry. Once you've identified it, create a six-month plan to deal with it.

Then, examine the other trends you short-listed in the "Get Practical" section above and design a one- to two-year plan to address each of the obstacles.

WHAT ARE WE ACTUALLY WILLING TO CHANGE?

I saved the most difficult conversation until last. You can have every conversation listed in the previous chapters, but if you're not willing to change, you've wasted your time and your breath. The honest truth is, most churches, people, and organizations struggle with change.

Change is hard because by default, we cling to the status quo. Typically, people change when the pain associated with the status quo becomes greater than the pain associated with change. In many churches, as long as the bills are being paid and people are still showing up, the motivation to change remains too low to really push ahead on the issues discussed in this book and the other issues facing the church. The motivation to change is even lower if you are experiencing momentum. Many leaders in growing organizations don't want to jeopardize success. As a result, the greatest threat to your future success in leadership is often your current success.

I'm writing this chapter because I'm hoping your church will be different. The majority of the conversations in this book focus on changes that are happening outside the church in the wider culture. If the change inside the church isn't equal to or greater than the change outside our walls, greater irrelevance is inevitable.

While that thought can be somewhat depressing, think of the flip side. History belongs to the innovators. It belongs to the leaders who dared to dream, to try things no one else was trying, to experiment, to push the boundaries of what everyone else believed was possible. As Henry Ford famously said, "If I had asked people what they wanted, they would have said faster horses." Or as Steve Jobs put it, "A lot of the time people don't know what they want until you show it to them."[41] If you are prepared to tackle change with a fully engaged heart, you can help not only your church but maybe even *the* church better accomplish the mission before us.

Perhaps that reminder is all some of you need: just a reminder to be bold and to accomplish what you have been called to accomplish. For many leaders, though, change is a frightening prospect. So in this chapter, I'll share some insights from two church leaders who have led change effectively in fairly resistant settings. I'll also offer some practical strategies you can use if your church seems resistant to change. I will conclude the chapter by offering some practical advice to leaders who want to lead change but who themselves are not senior leaders—a situation that requires skill to navigate.[42]

While there is much to be said about change, let's begin with some insights gleaned from Ron Edmondson and Dom Ruso, two pastors who have led established churches through change with considerable effectiveness.

HOW TO NAVIGATE CHANGE IN A TRADITIONAL CHURCH: RON EDMONDSON'S STORY

How do you navigate change when your context is traditional—really traditional? Sometimes the very idea can seem impossible. That was the challenge facing Ron Edmondson, whom I interviewed in episode 10 of my leadership podcast.[43] Ron assumed leadership of 105-year-old Immanuel Baptist Church in Lexington, Kentucky, a church that had plateaued at around 1,000 attenders and had been at that level for years. In addition, the average age of the congregation was considerably older than the community. In his first three years of leadership, weekend attendance grew from 1,000 to more than 2,400, and the church experienced an influx of young families.

A few things helped Ron establish the groundwork for change. First, Ron and the leadership at Immanuel established a very clear understanding of what Ron's mandate as pastor would be. In Ron's words, their understanding was that "this was a church that had seen better days and wanted to see better days again, so that's why I'm here." To do that, Ron looked for connection points with the past: "I've tried to be very intentional about embracing the culture that's here without erasing it. I'm embracing the history and the success of this church and reminding them that they've been through tremendous change in the last hundred years that has shaped who this church is today, and that's what we're doing again."

Next, Ron and his staff made some Sunday morning shifts that made their ministry more effective. "We had a contemporary service that was early and a more blended service later. I don't understand why they did that. The people you're trying to reach early don't get up early. And we switched those, which was a small change in my mind. It was a monumental change around here, but it was probably the single greatest thing in allowing us to grow with young families again."

Ron also refocused the church's language as he encouraged people to talk about what was happening outside of the church walls rather than only what was happening inside the congregation. He focused the language around their vision to make it more memorable. "We put some strategy words around it: gather, grow, and serve. And we have talked about those continually. In fact, I don't think you could find somebody who's been here longer than two or three weeks who doesn't know we talk about gather, grow, and serve."

With those simple changes, the church doubled in a year. Ron said the growth has been primarily unchurched families, which is their goal. They also met their budget and saw leadership gaps filled.

A few other things helped Ron and the team find momentum as well. They became more visible in the community through outreach, which gave the church more of a profile than it used to have. Ron also changed the congregation's language around outreach from "invite a friend" to "bring a friend" (something they learned from another church). Ron notes it's changing "how [people are] viewing their workplace and how they're viewing their neighborhoods, and what their role is in leading people to Jesus and nurturing them in their faith." In line with what Kara Powell suggests in *Sticky Faith*, the congregation has been looking for ways to bridge the gap between the seniors and the young families, who make up most of their growth. Bridging these two worlds can help turn potential division into potential unity.

Ron also faced his share of challenges in this role. Leading change on this scale is not for the faint of heart. Candidly, Ron admitted that despite the growth they experienced, he still received more criticism than praise. "It's just the way it was, and I think you've got to know that if you're coming into this, that that's going to be part of it. And then I have a church with very little filter, when it comes to that, among some of the people. So knowing that coming in, that that was a real possibility."

So how has Ron dealt with the opposition? "You just keep going back to the calling and the same way, hopefully, you do with the positives. You don't store them up and say, 'Look what I've done.' You don't store up the criticism and say, 'Look what I've done wrong.' And I think it's the exact same approach. It's recognizing, asking yourself, 'Is this true? Is there something here I need to learn from? Is this representative? Is it larger?' Seek affirmation among the people God sent you to minister to, not the people who weren't going to 'get it' anyway."

Ron had to come to terms with the fact that the pace of change in a traditional setting would be slower than in a church plant. "I have to adapt the change to the environment that I have here, which is gonna be slower, which is gonna mean that I have to communicate more often, I have to bring more people along, I have to have more meetings before the meetings, that sort of thing. It's labor-some," he said.

While change will be hard, Ron's story also shows it's worth it, and that much is possible even in a short window of time in a traditional setting. Dom Ruso in Sarnia, Ontario, discovered the same thing.

HOW TO TURN AROUND A DECLINING CHURCH WITHOUT BLOWING IT APART: DOM RUSO'S STORY

Dom Ruso is another pastor who accepted the invitation to help an established church move out of decline. Unlike Ron Edmondson, Dom was not a church planter. He'd been in a teaching pastor role and felt God leading him to a church-transitioning context. Like Ron, he saw significant growth in the first three years of his leadership—attendance grew from 400 to more than 800 in a city of fewer than 100,000 people. (Dom tells his whole story in episode 15 of my leadership podcast.[44])

Dom realized that when it came to change, he had to learn from the past but not live in it. Like Ron Edmondson, Dom saw that the congregation had embraced change in the past, even if it had forgotten that for a season. Rather brilliantly, Dom sat down with the man who planted the church seventy-five years ago (yes, he was still alive). He brought a video crew and asked the founding pastor what his original vision was. Dom surprised the congregation with the video during their seventy-fifth anniversary, which took place months after Dom became their lead pastor: "I surprised the church and the leadership with that interview that I had with Dr. W. Hal McBain." Dr. McBain shared stories of challenges and encouraged Dom to take the church where God was calling them. "What's beautiful about Dr. McBain is his leadership and even his wisdom just constantly stayed away from the dangers of living in the past." Sharing the founder's story and vision with the congregation built trust for Dom.

Despite the growth, Dom also had to navigate pushback. Within a year of becoming the senior pastor, Dom faced the closure of a Christian school long associated with the church. While it was perhaps the right decision for the church, it was by no means universally popular. Dom realized that one key to leading change in that highly divisive situation was understanding that he had to pastor both "groups" equally (those for and those against), no matter what his personal opinion was. "I intentionally just prayed for them to be able to see that myself and our elders were doing everything we could to have the church's best interest in mind regularly."

Dom also came to terms with the fact that opposition to change is inevitable and unavoidable. "One of the things that I was learning is that as the church grew, the pushback came because people needed to grieve the fact that their old church was gone." Dom said he listened and acknowledged their grief, letting them know it's okay to grieve. He also decided to preach on change, drawing parallels between his congregation and the first-century church: "The church from its inception had to work through changes that caused this type of tension."

Finally, Dom realized he had to keep his eye on accomplishing the mission, not simply on the growth or success of the church. "I think the breakthrough is that God is doing something in you as the leader and something in your people on the journey toward breakthrough. If breakthrough is the goal, then you just force your way to get to the breakthrough because that's the goal."

While many leaders think change in a traditional context isn't possible, clearly it is. Change is more than possible, even if it's difficult.

WHAT TO DO WHEN PEOPLE WANT A CHURCH TO GROW ... BUT NOT CHANGE

As you position your church for future impact, your team will face numerous tensions. One problem many leaders who want to see change encounter is this: people who say (in as many words): *I want our church to grow. I just don't want it to change.* On the one hand, that's completely understandable. We all wish we could lose ten pounds while eating cheeseburgers, but life (and our bodies) simply doesn't work that way. Part of your job as a leader is realizing how absurd that line of thinking is, even if it is seductive. While it's difficult to know what to do when people want your church to grow but not change, the best place to start is with honest conversation. As you lead that conversation, here are six things to keep in mind:

1. Tell the truth.

Usually we hire trainers, coaches, counselors, and consultants to tell us the truth we can't see or, often, already know but won't face. That's my job and your job as the leader of an organization: we need to help people see the truth. Our job is to communicate the truth in love. Most church leaders will tilt toward love and compromise truth. In leadership, it's a mistake to compromise either. You must lead a truthful dialogue.

So what's the truth about wanting to grow but not wanting to change? It's quite simple. *Your patterns, habits, and level of effectiveness as a church got you to where you are now.* If you want your current level of effectiveness, keep doing what you're doing right now. If you don't want your current level of effectiveness, *change.* It actually isn't much more complicated than that. Sometimes great leadership is as simple as pointing out the truth that nobody else wants to talk about. So above all, keep the dialogue honest.

2. Plot trajectory.

Learning how to plot trajectory is one of the best skills a leader can bring to the table. Plotting trajectory is simply mapping out the probable course or path an organization, person, or object is on. This is critical because usually, when it comes to people and organizations, we're not sure where we're headed.

To plot trajectory, ask two questions: If we continue doing what we're doing today, where will we be one year, two years, and five years from now? If we change, where will we be one year, two years, and five years from now? You may not know for sure where you'll end up, but if you start asking the question, you'll be amazed at what you discover. Try it.

3. Ban delusional talk.

This is related to keeping the conversation honest, but it takes it a level deeper. Those of us who resist change are often delusional. *I can continue to be rude to my spouse and our marriage will get better. I can slack off at work and get a better performance review. I can get abs of steel in a workout that lasts sixty seconds.* Most of us become crazy people when we're fighting change. So, as a leader, ban delusional talk around your table. Call it out. In love, let people see how crazy their thinking really is.

> *I understand you think your program is amazing, but it has an attendance of three. What do you suggest we do about that?*

> *I know you love Southern Gospel music, but most of the teens we want to reach don't.*

> *I realize you love our organization just the way it is, but the average age of our attenders is sixty-five, and we're missing the younger families we're called to reach.*

> *I know you think a new building will solve all our problems, but why can't we solve them in our current, half-empty facility?*

Don't let your leaders be delusional. Refuse to allow people to divorce themselves from reality.

4. Get an outside view.

Familiarity breeds contempt and distorts perspective. If your team doesn't immediately respond healthily to a call for change, you might be ripe for an outside voice to help you arrive at a new place. This would be the perfect time to read a book together (or more broadly share a chapter of this one), attend a conference, or hire a consultant. If the future is at stake, it's not a bad investment to spend the money on an outside perspective.

5. Offer constant feedback.

As you move through these conversations, keep people honest. It will be hard. But you need to do this. Continue to point the group back to the truth. Honestly, gracefully, but truthfully. Just keep snapping people back to reality. I say this because it will require Herculean effort to ensure you don't end up hoping for a diet-pill-and-cupcake solution. When it comes to change, there is little gain without significant pain.

6. Draw a line and call it what it is.

At some point you have to stop talking and start doing. Here's my suggestion. If you've been in an honest dialogue for six months and are not making progress (that is, you haven't made a plan for change you are ready to act on), you have come to a moment of truth. At some point, you just need to tell everyone where you have landed:

So our plan for change is to implement X, Y, and Z by this date. Let's do it!

Or

So essentially we have decided that we will not grow. We are content with the status quo. We will not change. And we will live with the consequences of stagnation, decline, and decay.

Guess what? Ninety-nine percent of leaders will never utter the second statement. And that's why they're stuck. That's why they're perpetually frustrated. But that second statement is exactly what you need to say if that's your reality. And then—are you ready?—you need to decide whether you still want to lead that organization. Many leaders stay on, hoping for change without any realistic plan for change and without facing the hard reality that change probably isn't going to happen. That's a recipe for frustration, cynicism, and even burnout. Conversely, you might decide you are not called to lead a church that wants to change, in which case the fit will be fine. But drawing a line and calling things what they are is critical to obtaining clarity. At least you then know what you're dealing with.

HOW TO GET ALIGNMENT AROUND THE CHANGE YOU WANT TO MAKE

People always ask me, "What's the key to leading change?" (as if there were *one* secret that made change happen every time). Of course, there is no "one secret" to change. If it were simple, there would be far more stories of widespread change in churches—and even in organizations—than there are.

And yet, personally speaking, there is *one* thing that has helped me more than anything else in almost twenty years of leading change. This one thing has not only helped me immensely in leading others through change; it's helped me stay motivated in seasons where I've felt like packing it in as I've led change in traditional and nontraditional settings.

So what is this one thing? It's this: focusing on the *why*, not on the *how* and *what*.

If you think about it, there are really only three issues that come up around any leadership table: what, how, and why.

What are we going to do?

How are we going to do it?

Why are we doing it?

Most leaders intuitively focus on the *what* and the *how*, neglecting the *why*. That's the mistake. And here's why that's a bad idea.

What and *how* are inherently divisive.

Why, on the other hand, unites people.

Let's break that down a little further. Spend any time in leadership and it won't take you long to see that people usu-ally disagree on *what*. One person likes a certain style of music. Someone else likes another. One person wants to paint a room gray; someone else likes taupe. One demographic prefers earlier services; another likes late morning best. Your team thinks you should spend the money. The other team disagrees. *What* is inherently divisive.

How is often just as divisive. Even when people agree on *what,* as soon as the discussion goes further, people start asking: *So, exactly how are we going to pay for this? How will we get people on board? How can you be certain this is going to work? How long will all of this take?* Great dreams can easily end up dashed on the rocks over details as small as timing and budget.

So what do you do when your vision for the future begins to disintegrate as the discussion moves to *what* and *how?* You do one thing: you refocus the conversation on *why.* When people begin to dispute the changes, redirect the conversation by saying something like: *Let's think about why we're doing this in the first place. It's to reach our community, and I'm confident we can make an impact if we all pull together.* Feel the mood in the room shift?

Here are some other phrases that can steer a conversation back to the why:

> *Because we imagine a church that our kids and grandkids want to come to.*

> *Because we want to be a church our friends love to attend.*

> *Because we want to be a place where people who don't feel welcome today feel welcome tomorrow.*

Because we love Christ and the world for which he died.

Because we have a passion for those who don't yet know Christ.

Because our current methods aren't optimally helping us accomplish our mission.

It's hard to disagree with statements like these, isn't it? That's because *why* appeals to the best in people. Consequently, when you focus on why, you often find people rallying to a cause that's bigger than themselves, that's truthfully bigger than all of us. And that only makes sense. Most people are actually a part of your church because at some point, they decided to give their lives to Christ and become part of a higher cause. Your job is to remind them (and yourself) of this daily.

Leaders who relentlessly refocus on the *why* are always the most effective leaders.

If the entire group stays focused on the *why,* the *what* and the *how* have a way of working themselves out far more easily because *why* motivates.

When people agree on the why, the conversation starts to sound more like this:

Well, I might not like it personally, but it is the most sensible approach. Let's go for it.

We'll find the money somewhere.

Let's give it a try. I'll put my objections aside.

I feel like there's a future again!

Will you get some opposition? You bet. But if a few people leave ... let them go. They can always find another church to attend. The people you'll reach will likely far outnumber the people you lose.[45]

HOW TO LEAD CHANGE WHEN YOU'RE NOT THE SENIOR LEADER

One more thing before we close this conversation on change—this time for any of you reading this book who are not senior leaders. You may be at the point where you realize you face the formidable task of trying to convince a resistant senior leader or leadership team that it's time to change. My guess is if you've read this far as the lone wolf on your team, you're now depressed. You have all this energy and excitement about change, but it's accompanied by a sinking feeling that no one in your church is going to buy in. Sadly, this happens far more than it ought to.

What do you do if you want to see change and you're not a senior leader? It's easy to think you're powerless or to try to work around a leader you disagree with. But neither is a great strategy. So how do you "lead up" without being subversive or ineffective?

Think Like a Senior Leader
Effecting change when you're not the senior leader begins with you imagining how you would feel if you *were* the senior leader. Try to get in that head space, even if it feels like

a stretch. Imagine the pressures and unique challenges facing your senior leader. I promise you there are many: the reality of reporting to a governing board, to the staff, and perhaps to the congregation; budget restraints; the challenges of balancing all the needs of the church's various ministries and groups; and the pastor's own personal views, convictions, and opinions on the issue. Once you've started to identify the issues he or she is facing, you can approach the conversation empathetically. Show him or her that you understand that they're in a sensitive position and that you're willing to be open and even flexible on some points.

As a senior leader, let me disclose a bias here. When someone on my team comes to me with any idea and I realize they have thought it through cross-organizationally (that is, they've thought through how it impacts the *entire* organization), I am far more open to it than otherwise. Why? Because

they're thinking about more than just themselves;

they did their homework;

they helped me do my homework;

they showed me they're leading at the next level.

I always try to be open to new ideas, but here's the truth. Often before the person is done with their presentation or we're done with the discussion, I've already thought through fifteen implications of their idea. If they show me they thought through the fifteen implications before they got to my office, I tend to be more impressed and, as a result, more open. I'm not saying that's a good thing; I'm just saying it's a true thing. And I think it's true of most senior leaders. When you think like a senior leader, you're more likely to persuade a senior leader.

Once you've determined an appropriate approach, here are some other factors to remember.

Express Desires, Not Demands

No one likes a demanding person. In fact, when someone demands something, there's something inside most of us that wants to *not* give them what they asked for. Leaders don't always follow that impulse, but expressing demands damages relationships. Instead, talk about what you *desire*. Show respect and tell your leader how *you* feel—don't tell your leader how you think *he* should feel. And above all, don't be demanding.

Explain the Why Behind the What

As we've seen above and as Simon Sinek has so rightly pointed out, people don't buy what you do; they buy why you do it.[46] Your best argument is not the *what* ("we need to completely transform our church") or the *how* ("here's how you should do it"). It's the *why* ("I think I've discovered a more effective way to reach families in our community and help parents win at home … can I talk to you about that?"). The more you explain the *why*, the more people will be open to the *what* and the *how*.

Stay Publicly Loyal

Andy Stanley phrases it this way: public loyalty buys you private leverage. It's true. If you start complaining to others about how resistant your senior leader is, that not only compromises your personal integrity, but also your senior leader's not clueless. He'll probably hear about it and he will lose respect for you. In my mind as a senior leader, the team members who conduct themselves like a cohesive team always have the greatest private influence. Your public loyalty will buy you private leverage.

Be a Part of the Solution

If you're discontent, it's not that difficult to drift into the category of critic. Unless, that is, you decide to be part of the solution. Offer help. Don't end-run your leader; run *with* your leader on the project.

> Be the most helpful you can be.
>
> Offer to do the legwork.
>
> Bring your best ideas to the table every day.

Ask yourself this: What can *I* change? You're in charge of something. Change it. You might argue that you don't have permission to change anything. Sure, you do. You can change your attitude. To some extent, you can change the culture of whatever you're in charge of. Think about it: if you're in charge of a volunteer team of five, make them the five best-loved people in the church or organization. Create a super-healthy team. Accomplish all you can accomplish. Do everything you're capable of doing. Others might sit up and take notice, realizing everyone would be better off if they did what you're doing.

And even if no one notices, the five people you work with will notice. And they'll be thankful for it.

If you won't be part of the solution, you'll eventually become part of the problem. So be part of the solution.

Change Yourself

You're human. You'll be tempted to focus only on the changes you'd like to see in others. But the best leaders also see a great opportunity in a stalemate. As I hinted earlier, great leaders focus on changing themselves. A stalemate is a chance to grow in character and skill. If you become the healthiest, most self-aware member of the team, people will be attracted to you and what you have to say. And you won't be as busy trying to change them. Which might be a nice turn of events in some cases.

CHANGE IS DIFFICULT, BUT WORTH IT

Given the massive shift happening in our culture, the ability to navigate change is sure to emerge as one of the key leadership skills required over the next few decades. Church teams that want to see a better future will not only be committed to changing things; they will become students of how to navigate change.

Mastering the art of leading change is an essential skill for any leader motivated by even a single leadership objective discussed in this book; without change, there is no point. So before you put this book down, decide what you want to change, and then begin to discuss how you will go about changing it. As difficult as that is, the mission is too important to do otherwise.

Conversation #7

DISCUSSION QUESTIONS

Talk About It

1. Does your church easily embrace change? If so, why? If not, why not? What keeps you from seeing change as a friend rather than an enemy?

2. As you read through Ron Edmondson's and Dom Ruso's stories, what encourages you? Does anything frighten you about the pace of change adopted by both leaders?

3. Of all the things associated with change, which frightens you the most?

4. Has your church ever tolerated "delusional talk"? What makes you tolerate it?

5. What's the trajectory of your church within five years if you don't change? What is it if you do change? Ask the same questions again but use a ten-year timeline.

6. In your conversations about change, do you tend to focus on the *why*, or more on the *what* or the *how*? Are your conversations working for you or against you as a result?

7. If you're reading this book and you're not the senior leader, what was the biggest insight you read that can help you lead change more effectively within your organization?

Get Practical

Work through this list of six things a leader can do when people want their church to grow but not change. Create an honest assessment of how your church is doing in each area. Some of the things listed below describe a culture and some are action steps, but each should give you a gauge of where your church truly is when it comes to having an honest conversation and action plan around change.

1. Tell the truth.

2. Plot trajectory.

3. Ban delusional talk.

4. Get an outside view.

5. Offer constant feedback.

6. Draw a line and call it what it is.

Make It Happen

Identify the single biggest obstacle to change in your church. Once you've identified it, create a six-month plan to remove it.

In addition, identify two to five other key obstacles to change. Now design a one- to two-year plan to address each of the obstacles.

For further information on leading change, see my book *Leading Change Without Losing It: Five Strategies That Can Revolutionize How You Lead Change When Facing Opposition* (reThink, 2012).

CONCLUSION

Leadership is so demanding that many leaders only give passing thought to the broader issues facing the church. If you've made it this far in the conversation, clearly you're not that kind of leader. For that I'm incredibly grateful.

We need a generation of church leaders who are committed to taking on the challenges before us, not just to working in the daily tasks of ministry. And that takes, among other things, courage, time, and stamina. It's energy well invested though. While many leaders would say they don't have time for the kinds of conversations contemplated by a book like this, I often find that leaders who take the time to process the bigger issues tend to have growing churches. There's some kind of correlation between leaders who take the time to think through big issues and leaders who lead effective ministries.

If you find yourself on the front end of that process (maybe this is the first time you've ever sat down as a team to discuss any bigger issues), be encouraged. I believe the time you've invested will pay off in some beautiful ways moving forward. It has paid for me and many other leaders I know.

Although we find ourselves in challenging days, I believe the best years of the church are ahead of us. Every time there is a change in history, there's potential to gain and potential to lose. I believe the potential to gain is greater than the potential to lose. Why? As despairing or as cynical as some might be (sometimes understandably) over the church's future, we have to remind ourselves that the church was Jesus' idea, not ours. It will survive our missteps and whatever cultural trends happen around us. We certainly don't always get things right, but Christ has an incredible history of pulling together Christians in every generation to share his love for a broken world. As a result—to paraphrase Mark Twain—the reports of the church's death are greatly exaggerated. The best is yet to come, and you have the potential to play a meaningful part in that amazing story.

NOTES

CHAPTER 1

1. "Small Churches Struggle to Grow Because of the People They Attract," Barna Group, September 2, 2003, https://www.barna.org/barna-update /article/5-barna-update/126-small-churches-struggle-to-grow-because -of-the-people-they-attract#.VR7fg1zWJ0o.

2. Although it's twenty years old, this is still the best book I know on the subject of delegation: Carl F. George and Warren Bird, *How to Break Growth Barriers: Capturing Overlooked Opportunities for Church Growth* (Grand Rapids, MI: Baker Books, 1993).

3. North Point church has done a good job at creating small groups, and they share their strategy here: http://inside northpoint.org/groups/.

4. This post by Jeff Brodie about what church constitutions need to have is so helpful: http://www.jeffbrodie.com/5-essentials-every-church -constitution-needs-in-the-future/.

5. Andy Stanley has a great podcast on steps instead of programs at http:// insidenorthpoint.org/practically-speaking/.

6. If you want to read more about change, I wrote *Leading Change Without Losing It* (you can find it at http://orangebooks.com/books/leading -change-without-losing-it). Additionally, John Kotter's *Leading Change* is a must-read classic (Harvard Business Review Press, 2012).

Chapter 2

7. Alicia Parlapiano, Robert Gebeloff, and Shan Carter, "The Shrinking American Middle Class," *The Upshot* (blog), January 26, 2015, http:// www.nytimes.com/interactive/2015/01/25/upshot/shrinking-middle -class.html?_r=0&abt=0002&abg=1.

8. US Personal Disposable Income: http://www.tradingeconomics.com /united-states/disposable-personal-income. Canada Personal Disposable Income: http://www.tradingeconomics.com/canada/disposable-personal -income.

9. Amy Langfield, "Leisure Travel Rising Among Road Trippers and Jetsetters," CNBC, March 5, 2014, http://www.cnbc.com /id/101395861#.

10. Gabe Lyons and David Kinnaman have outlined helpful characteristics of unchurched people in *UnChristian* (Grand Rapids, MI: Baker, 2007), and David tackled the subject again in *You Lost Me* (Grand Rapids, MI: Baker, 2011). I won't repeat those characteristics here.

11. This idea is from Andy's talk at the Drive conference, which I blogged about here: http://careynieuwhof.com/2013/03/21-key-learnings-from -andy-stanley-and-the-drive-conference/.

12. My podcast interview with Will Mancini is episode 23 at https://itunes .apple.com/us/podcast/id912753163.

13. See Bob Goff, *Love Does: Discover a Secretly Incredible Life in an Ordinary World* (Nashville, TN: Thomas Nelson, 2012). Follow Bob on Twitter at https://twitter.com/bobgoff.

14. Aaron Smith and Monica Anderson, "5 Facts About Online Dating," Pew Research Center, April 20, 2015, http://www.pewresearch.org/fact -tank/2015/04/20/5-facts-about-online-dating/.

15. See episode 23 of my podcast at https://itunes.apple.com/us/podcast /id912753163.

16. Caleb K. Bell, "Poll: Americans love the Bible but don't read it much," Religion News Service, April 4, 2013, http://www.religionnews. com/2013/04/04/poll-americans-love-the-bible-but-dont-read-it-much/.

Chapter 3

17. I wrote a blog post about dealing with cynicism: http://careynieuwhof .com/2013/03/how-do-you-kill-the-cynicism-inside-you/.

18. My podcast interview with Perry Noble is episode 2 at https://
itunes.apple.com/us/podcast/id912753163.

19. Here are some ideas for refreshing your devotional time: http://
careynieuwhof.com/2012/12/how-to-kickstart-your-devotional-life/.

20. Here's why I think sleep is one of the most underrated leadership secret
weapons there is: http://careynieuwhof.com/2014/10/sleep-secret
-leadership-weapon-one-wants-talk/.

21. I wrote a post on time management that links to many time
management tips: http://careynieuwhof.com/2013/03/why-you-cant
-have-5-minutes-of-my-time/.

Chapter 5

22. My podcast interview with Kara Powell is episode 4 at https://
itunes.apple.com/us/podcast/id912753163.

23. Kara's books and more resources are at http://stickyfaith.org/leader
/store.

24. "Americans Divided on the Importance of Church," Barna.org, March
25, 2014, https://www.barna.org/barna-update/culture/661-americans
-divided-on-the-importance-of-church#.UzwMlq1dW7o.

25. The videocast of our Skeptics Wanted series is here: https://
itunes.apple.com/ca/podcast/connexus-church-video-podcast
/id843290736?mt=2.

26. If you want to read more, I outlined how to write a message series for
unchurched people here: http://careynieuwhof.com/2013/09/how
-to-design-a-message-series-for-unchurched-people. In addition, my
friends at Preaching Rocket offer a free online conference that can help
anyone become a better communicator: http://therocketcompany.com
/preaching/.

27. Find out more about Orange at http://thinkorange.com. Find *Lead
Small Culture* (Cumming, GA: reThink, 2014) at http://orangebooks.
com/books/creating-a-lead-small-culture and *Lead Small* (reThink,
2013) at http://orangebooks.com/books/lead-small.

28. "Five Trends Among the Unchurched," Barna.org, October 9, 2014, https://www.barna.org/barna-update/culture/685-five-trends-among -the-unchurched#.VNT9vofWJ0q.

29. I wrote a post about how to be an appropriately transparent leader without oversharing: http://careynieuwhof.com/2014/01/how-to-be-an -appropriately-transparent-leader-without-oversharing/.

30. Reggie Joiner, Orange Tour, Fall 2014.

31. Jim Collins, "Confront the Brutal Facts (Yet Never Lose Faith)," *Good to Great*, ch. 4 (New York: HarperCollins, 2001).

Chapter 6

32. Dan Schawbel, "Andy Molinsky: How to Adapt to Cultural Changes in Foreign Countries," *Forbes.com,* April 10, 2013, http://www.forbes.com /sites/danschawbel/2013/04/10/andy-molinsky-how-to-adapt-to -cultural-changes-in-foreign-countries/.

33. SyncForce, "Ranking the Brands Top 100, 2015," rankingthebrands. com, http://www.rankingthebrands.com/The-Brand-Rankings. aspx?rankingID=30.

34. Rich Birch has a great infographic on how legacy is becoming a liability: http://www.unseminary.com/how-global-consumer-trends-are -impacting-your-church-infographic/.

35. I wrote a blog post about the importance of having younger leaders here: http://careynieuwhof.com/2012/10/why-young-leadership-is-essential -to-your-organization/.

36. You can see an example of one of North Point's sermon series microsites here: http://preparedseries.org.

37. Edmund Lee, "TV Subscriptions Fall for First Time as Viewers Cut the Cord," *Bloomberg Business* (blog), March 19, 2014, http:// www.bloomberg.com/news/articles/2014-03-19/u-s-pay-tv -subscriptions-fall-for-first-time-as-streaming-gains.

38. This Leadership Network article has some interesting stats on megachurch attendance: http://leadnet.org/9-fascinating-facts-about-people-who-attend-megachurches/.

39. See Thom Rainer's interesting blog post titled "Ten Ways Millennials Are Shaping Local Congregations Today," August 13, 2014, at http://thomrainer.com/2014/08/13/ten-ways-millennials-shaping-local-congregations-today/.

40. Find Rich Birch at http://www.unseminary.com.

Chapter 7

41. Andy Reinhardt, "Steve Jobs: 'There's Sanity Returning,'" *Business Week*, May 25, 1998, http://www.businessweek.com/1998/21/b3579165.htm.

42. Beyond what I share in this chapter, if you anticipate a congregation or group that will resist the changes you're proposing, I outline five strategies to help you lead change in the face of opposition in my book *Leading Change Without Losing It* (Cumming, GA: reThink, 2012).

43. My podcast interview with Ron Edmondson is episode 10 at https://itunes.apple.com/us/podcast/id912753163.

44. My podcast interview with Dom Ruso is episode 15 at https://itunes.apple.com/us/podcast/id912753163.

45. For more on the math of leading change through opposition, see my book *Leading Change Without Losing It* (Cumming, GA: reThink, 2012).

46. Simon Sinek explores the importance of why at https://www.startwithwhy.com.

ABOUT THE AUTHOR

Carey Nieuwhof is the lead pastor of Connexus Church, a growing, multi-campus church north of Toronto and a strategic partner of North Point Community Church. Before starting Connexus, Carey served for twelve years in a mainline church, transitioning three small congregations into a single, rapidly growing church.

He speaks to North American and global leaders about leadership, change, personal growth, and parenting.

Carey writes one of the most widely read Christian leadership blogs today and hosts *The Carey Nieuwhof Leadership Podcast,* on which he interviews today's best Christian leaders. Carey is the author of *Leading Change Without Losing It* and coauthor of *Parenting Beyond Your Capacity.* He and his wife, Toni, live near Barrie, Ontario, and have two sons.

Follow Carey on Twitter @CNieuwhof and on the web at www.CareyNieuwhof.com.